MOSCOW

2010

ЯРКИЙ ГОРОД

Text by Tatyana Vishnevskaya

Translated from the Russian by Valery Fateyev

Photographs by Alexander Zakharchenko,

Sergei Zakharchenko and Nikolai Rakhmanov

Edited by Yevgeny Andreyev and Natalia Morozova

Design by Alexander Rodionov

Computer layout by Meta Leif

Technical Director Peter Krakovsky

Colour correction by Liubov Bogdanova,

Inna Zezegova and Tatyana Chernyshenko

ISBN 5-9663-0059-3

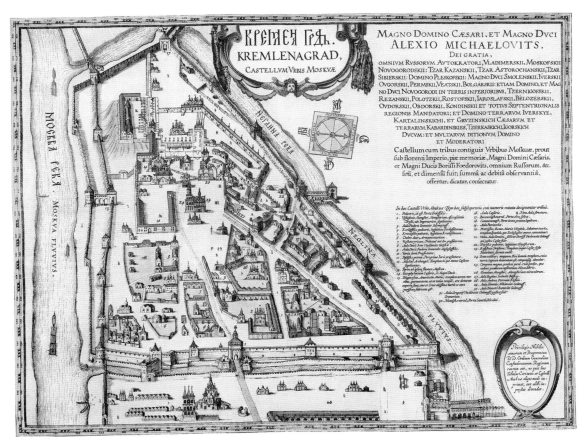

"The Kremlin Town". **Plan of the Kremlin. Early 1600s**

"To visit Moscow means to know Russia," wrote the great Russian historian Nikolai Karamzin. Since time immemorial golden-domed Moscow has been regarded as the heart of Russia, the focus of the Russian spirit and a symbol of Russian statehood.

In 2007 the city will celebrate its jubilee. 865 years have passed since the memorable day of 4 April 1147 when Yury Dolgoruky, the Prince of Suzdal, gave a feast on his estate in honour of Sviatoslav Olgovich, the Prince of Seversk, inviting him there with the words: "Come, brother, to me to Moscow." This is the first mention of Moscow in the Chronicles and it is thought to be the date of its foundation. In 1328 the Moscow Prince Ivan Kalita received an edict from the Tatar Khan Uzbek for becoming the Grand Prince and thus the history of Moscow as the capital of Russia began. Towards the end of the fifteenth century Moscow grew into the political, spiritual and administrative centre of Russia, the bulwark of the country's political and spiritual power. The process continued until the early eighteenth century when Peter the Great built a new capital, St Petersburg, on the shore of the Gulf of Finland. Deprived of its status of the capital, Moscow, however, did not lose its spiritual, economic and cultural significance. In 1918 the newest period in the history of the city began: Moscow became the capital of the new, Soviet state. Moscow is today a multi-million megapolis, the capital of the Russian Federation, ranking the fifth among the world's capitals as regards its population.

THE MOSCOW KREMLIN

The ancient Chronicles have brought to us legends and real stories about the beautiful white-stone city standing on seven hills that had risen amidst a dense forest with the glistening of golden domes of its countless churches, under the powerful protection of its mighty fortified walls. Indeed, like any medieval city, Moscow began with a fortress. The Moscow Kremlin, the most ancient and central part of the capital, one of the richest architectural complexes in the world, soars on Borovitsky Hill, on the left bank of the Moskva River. Over the years it has changed its appearance several times, expanding its boundaries, strengthening and improving itself.

Ancient archaeological finds on the Kremlin territory date from the second millennium B.C. The original settlement that occupied only about 1.5 hectares in the south-western extremity of Kremlin Hill, in 1145 was fenced with the earliest wooden walls and in 1156 strengthened with an earthen rampart. A trade area, the future Red Square, took shape under the protection of the fortress. The first stone walls were erected in 1367 under Dmitry Donskoi and the area of the Kremlin was then enlarged nearly to its present-day dimensions. In the second half of the

fifteenth century the old white-stone walls grew decrepit and partly broke down. Ivan III invited for the restoration of the Kremlin a group of Italian architects, Antonio Gilardi, Marco Ruffo, Pietro Antonio Solari and Aloisio da Carcano, with Aristotle Fioravanti as their head. The citadel built by them in 1485–95 met the latest demands of fortification and it has survived with alterations to this day.

The Kremlin walls stretch for 2,235 metres and are 3.5 to 6.5 metres thick and 5 to 19 metres high. Following the outlines of Kremlin Hill, they form an irregular triangular. Rising over them are twenty towers, six of which — the Saviour, Nicholas, Trinity, Borovitskaya, Tayninskaya and Constantine-Helen Towers — have gateways. Originally the passage alongside the top of the walls and all the towers were covered with a wooden roof.

The Tayninskaya Tower, built the first in 1485, was provided with a gate and a secret passage to the river. Then, in 1485–88, two round corner towers, the Vodovzvodnaya (Water Supply) and Beklemishevskaya Towers – were started and the construction of the southern wall running along the Moskva River was completed. In the seventeenth century all the towers (except for the Nicholas

Giacomo Quarenghi. *Panoramic View of the Kremlin.* **1797**

Tower) were decorated with tent-shaped tops and the decorative Tsar Tower was erected on the eastern wall. In 1925 the wall facing Red Square became a burial place where urns with ashes of outstanding statesmen were immured. In 1935–37 five-cornered ruby stars replaced the double-headed copper eagles surviving from the pre-revolutionary period on the Saviour, Nicholas, Trinity, Borovitskaya and Vodovzvodnaya Towers.

The names of the Kremlin towers bring back the spirit of hoary antiquity. For instance, the Nabatnaya (Alarm Bell) Tower built in 1495 (height 38 m), received

View of the Kremlin and the Large Stone Bridge

its title from the bell hanging in its upper tier and informing the Muscovites about danger. The name of the corner Borovitskaya (Forest) Tower, through which people could get to the Tsar's palace, recalls the ancient times when a pine forest rustled in this area. And the Constantine-Helen Tower, square in plan (height 36.8 m), was named after the Church of St Constantine and St Helen that stood nearby. Pietro Antonio Solari built this tower in 1490 on the site of the gate through which the army of Dmitry Donskoi went to the Kulikovo Battle in 1380.

The Trinity Tower, built in 1490 by Aloisio da Carcano, is the only tower with a gateway on the side of the Alexander Garden. The six-storeyed tower, eighty metres high, has two basement floors intended originally for defensive purposes and later used as a prison. Leading to the Trinity Tower is a stone bridge of the same name with crenellated walls on either side. The entry to the bridge is marked by the Kutafya Tower (13.5 m high) – the only surviving defensive structure before a bridge at the Kremlin walls. This squat and crenellated tower, round in plan, owes its name to its appearance: *kutafya* meant an awkward, untidy woman in early times.

The Kremlin. The Constantine and Helen Tower, Alarm Clock Tower, Saviour Tower. 1490s
Architect: Pietro Antonio Solari. Tent-shaped tops: 17th century

The Kremlin. The Kutafya Tower. 1516. The Trinity Tower. 1495. Architect: Aloisio da Carcano

The Kremlin. The Saviour Tower. 1491, architect: Pietro Antonio Solari 1624–25, architect: Bazhen Ogurtsov

The Saviour (originally Frolovskaya) Tower with a gateway, erected in 1491 by the architect Pietro Antonio Solari, was named after the Vernicle icon of the Saviour placed over its gateway on the Kremlin side. The second in height after the Trinity Tower (71 m with its star), it has nine storeys with a tent-shaped top built by the Russian architect Bazhen Ogurtsov in 1624–25. The first clock appeared on the Saviour Tower in the second half of the sixteenth century. The present-day chiming clock, the fourth one in the history of the Kremlin, has been installed in 1770. Like before, the Saviour Gate serves today as the main, official entrance to the Kremlin. In olden times it was considered a holy gate and so it was not allowed to ride or walk through it with a covered head.

The Saviour Tower. Chiming clock

The Moscow Kremlin is an integral historical and architectural complex, on the territory of which are located wonderful monuments of Russian architecture of the fifteenth to nineteenth century. They make up two basic ensembles framing the main squares of the Kremlin – Cathedral Square and Ivanovskaya Square. The first of them (as its name suggests) was formed by the celebrated Kremlin cathedrals of the Dormition, the Annunciation and the Archangel Michael, as well as the Faceted Chamber with the Church of the Deposition of the Robe. Cathedral Square adjoins Ivanovskaya Square that lies to the east of the Ivan the Great Bell-Tower, from which it has received its name. Towards the seventeenth century Ivanovskaya Square, with buildings of various *prikazes* or ministries erected on it, became the administrative centre of the Kremlin, to which petitioners gathered from entire Russia. In order to out-voice the noise of a crowd, the *prikaz* officers who used to make public the Tsar's decrees, had to strain their lungs. It is believed that the widely used Russian expression to shout "all over Ivanovskaya" (i.e. at the top of one's voice) comes from this place.

Domes of the Kremlin cathedrals

Fiodor Alexeyev. *Cathedral Square in the Moscow Kremlin.* **Early 19th century**

13

The Cathedral of the Dormition was Russia's main cathedral for six centuries. It was here that the Grand Princes were crowned, the Tsars and Emperors enthroned, the hierarchs of the Russian Orthodox Church consecrated, the principal state documents declared and services performed before military campaigns and after their completion.

The earliest stone Cathedral of the Dormition, founded by the first Moscow Grand Prince Ivan Kalita, was consecrated in 1327. When at the end of the fifteenth century Grand Prince Ivan III, who unified all the Russian lands under the power of Moscow, conceived to build a new residence, he began with the construction of the Dormition Cathedral. The Italian architect Aristotle Fioravanti, invited by the Grand Prince, was offered to use as a model the ancient sacred shrine of the Russian Orthodoxy – the twelfth-century Cathedral of the Dormition in Vladimir.

**The Kremlin. Cathedral of the Dormition. 1475–79
Architect: Aristotle Fioravanti**

Cross on the façade of the Cathedral of the Dormition

Cathedral of the Dormition. The Tsarina's preaching place
17th century. Reconstructed in the 19th century

Cathedral of the Dormition
The Tsar's place of Ivan the Terrible. 1551

Within five years (from 1575 to 1579) Fioravanti created an architectural master-piece of world significance. The church is a traditional Russian cross-shaped domed structure, but some original features distinguish its interior. For the first time in Russian architecture the architect used round pillars instead of heavy rectangular pylons so that the inner space became vast and filled with light and air. The painted decor of the cathedral strikes one by its magnificence. The frescoes are arranged in keeping with the Russian Orthodox canons: the divine images are placed in the domes, the tops of the walls are given to Gospel subjects, two next tiers feature the Virgin cycle and the lower tier depicts the Seven Ecumenical Councils. The western wall bears the huge *Last Judgement*; saints and martyrs are depicted on the pillars. The immense iconostasis, built in 1653 and ranking with the richest in the world, contains a magnificent collection of icons from the twelfth to seventeenth century.

Cathedral of the Dormition. Interior

Cathedral of the Dormition. Icon: *St George.* **12th century. Novgorod**

Until the end of the seventeenth century the Cathedral of the Assumption served as a burial place of the leading clerics of the Russian Orthodox Church. Altogether it has nineteen burials marked by a rich canopy: to the left of the entrance are located the tombs of the Moscow Metropolitans, to the right are those of the Patriarchs. The cathedral also contains the relics of the holy bishops SS Peter, Philip and Jonas that are open for worship. The holy relics are kept in wooden reliquaries decorated with metal plaques.

Cathedral of the Dormition. Canopy over the shrine with relics of Patriarch Hermogenus. 17th century

The Kremlin. Cathedral of the Annunciation. 1485–89

The south-western part of Cathedral Square is adorned with a pyramid-shaped silhouette of the Annunciation Cathedral crowned with nine gilded domes. Unlike the Dormition Cathedral, which was the main church of the state, the Cathedral of the Annunciation, more modest in dimensions, became the home church of the Moscow grand princes. It was also used for keeping the treasury of the grand princes and later of the Tsar. The cathedral was erected by Russian architects on the basement of the church that had once stood on this site.

Cathedral of the Annunciation. View of the iconostasis

Cathedral of the Annunciation. Interior
Images of Byzantine Emperors Constantine and Helen
on the south-western pillar

The ceremony of the consecration of the Annunciation Cathedral took place in August 1489, but its present-day appearance was formed in the 1660s. The inner painted decor is a work of Feodosy, the son of Dionysius, done in 1508. Traditional subjects are supplemented with an Apocalyptic cycle, representations of the Byzantine Emperors and the Tree of Jesse representing the genealogies of Christ. Of great magnificence is the fifteenth-century iconostasis, which includes a number of icons painted by the outstanding Russian artists Theophanes the Greek, Andrei Rublev and Prochorus of Gorodets. One's attention is also attracted by the floor of the cathedral made of inlaid jasper of various shades.

Cathedral of the Annunciation
Theophanes the Greek. Icon: *St John the Forerunner*. 1405

Cathedral of the Annunciation
Iconostasis in the "Synaxis of the Archangel Gabriel" Chapel

The Kremlin. The Faceted Chamber. 1487–1591
Architects: Marco Ruffo, Pietro Antonio Solari

Cathedral Square is limited from the west by the Faceted Chamber — the earliest of the Moscow civil structures that have reached us. It was built by the Italian architects Marco Ruffo and Pietro Antonio Solari in 1487–91, under Grand Prince Ivan III. The main, eastern front of the building is decorated with the so-called "diamond rustication", that is faced with stone carved in a special way, hence the name – the Faceted Chamber. Thanks to its rich decor the building plays an important role in the formation of the architectural appearance of Cathedral Square. Once the chamber was a section of the extinct Kremlin Palace and served as a festive Throne Hall. Adjoining it from the west is the Holy Corridor to which leads the Red Porch. Demolished in the 1930s, it was re-created in 1992–94.

The palace is a one-pillar structure covered with four cross vaults, typical of Russian civil architecture of the fifteenth and sixteenth centuries.

The Faceted Chamber. Western wall. Portal   **The Faceted Chamber. Interior ▶**

The Faceted Chamber. *The First Princes, Rurik's Successors*
Painting of the eastern wall. 1882

The Tsarina's Golden Chamber. *Entry of St Dinara into Tabriz*
Painting of the northern wall. 17th century

The dimensions of this grandiose throne room – 495 square metres – are striking — for two centuries it remained the largest building in Russian architecture. It was here that the most solemn and crowded state receptions were held, victories of the Russian arms were celebrated and the Zemstvo Councils were held.

In the sixteenth century the walls and vaults of the Faceted Chamber were painted all over with frescoes, which later were destroyed by fire. In 1668 they were re-created by Simon Ushakov, the famous painter to the Tsar, but his works perished in fire. The paintings that have reached our times, were executed in 1881 by icon-painters from Palekh according to the inventory of subjects compiled by Ushakov.

In 1838–49, during the construction of the Great Kremlin Palace, the Faceted Chamber was integrated into the new complex of palace buildings with which the Holy Corridor was connected.

Nowadays the Faceted Chamber serves as a reception hall in the residence of the President of the Russian Federation.

The Tsarina's Golden Chamber
Painting of the vaults. 17th century. Detail

The Tsarina's Golden Chamber. Interior

The Kremlin. Cathedral of the Archangel Michael
1505–08. Architect: Aleviz the New

The first white-stone church named after the Archistrategus Michael, the patron of the Moscow princes and their army, was built in Moscow in 1333 by orders of Ivan Kalita. In 1505–08 the Italian architect Aleviz the New (Aloisio Lamberti da Montagnana), invited by Ivan III, erected the cathedral that stands in the Kremlin to this day. This is the most unusual building on Cathedral Square – it combines the traditional five-domed top of an ancient Russian cross-in plan domed church with the order system of Renaissance architecture. The appearance of the cathedral is notable for its especial ornate character: the *zakomaras* (semi-circular arched gables) are designed as huge sea-shells⊠ the northern and western portals are embellished with white-stone carving.

Cathedral of the Archangel Michael. Icon:
The Archangel Michael. **First decades of the 15th century**

Cathedral of the Archangel Michael
Canopy over the shrine of the murdered Tsarevich Demetrius

Cathedral of the Archangel Michael. General view of the tombs of the 14th to 16th century near the southern wall

**Cathedral of the Archangel Michael
Interior**

Until the eighteenth century the cathedral served as the burial place of the Moscow princes and Russian Tsars. Today it contains 47 burials, including the tombs of Ivan Kalita, the first Moscow Grand Prince, and Ivan the Terrible, the first Russian Tsar. The cathedral was decorated with frescoes for the first time under Ivan the Terrible to honour the power of the grand princes and Tsars and in 1652–66 it was frescoed anew by Russian craftsmen headed by Simon Ushakov.

The iconostasis of the Cathedral of the Archangel Michael was created in 1679–81, in the reign of Tsar Fiodor Romanov. Nearly all its icons were painted by artists of the Armoury. The earliest piece is the patronal icon of the Archangel Michael (1399) placed to the right of the Holy Gate – it was a part of the iconostasis in the earliest Archangel Church. Legend has it that it was painted in honour of the victory of the Russian army on the Kulikovo Field as a commission of Prince Dmitry Donskoi's widow.

Cathedral of the Archangel Michael. Ritual vessels from the burials of Tsar Ivan the Terrible, Tsarevich Ivan Ivanovich and Tsar Fiodor Ivanovich. 16th century

At the foot of the Ivan the Great Bell-Tower, on a stone pediment stands the Tsar Bell. The Russian masters Ivan and Mikhail Matorin cast it, the largest metal bell in the world, in 1733–35. It is more than 6 metres high, weighs over 200 tonnes and has a diameter of 6.6 metres. Not far from it, on Ivanovskaya Square, one can see another masterpiece of cast metalwork — the Tsar Cannon (1586), a 5-metre-long gun weighing about 40 tonnes, cast and richly decorated by the craftsman Andrei Chokhov.

The Kremlin. The Tsar Cannon. 1586
Made by Andrei Chokhov

The Kremlin. The Tsar Bell. 1733–35
Cast by Ivan and Mikhail Matorin

Domes of the Kremlin cathedrals ▶

The Terem Palace, one of the most picturesque structures in the Moscow Kremlin, seems to have come down from the pages of Russian fairy-tales. The style of this five-storey building decorated with white-stone carving is a variegated mixture of elements borrowed from Italian, Russian and Oriental architecture. In the lower part of the palace, built in 1487, originally housed the Tsar's workshop. The two upper tiers of the chambers, the third and fourth floors, were erected by the Russian architects Bazhen Ogurtsov, Antip Konstantinov, Trifon Sgarutin and Larion Ushakov.

The Terem Palace. 1635–36. Architects: Antip Konstantinov, Bazhen Ogurtsov, Trefil Sharutin, Larion Ushakov

The Terem Palace. The small golden-topped *terem* and the Watch Tower

The Terem Palace. The Bedchamber

**The Terem Palace
Passage to the circular gallery**

In the middle of the seventeenth century the palace became a permanent dwelling of the Russian Tsars. The royal apartments were on the third floor of the building. Today these interiors — the Entrance Room, the Refectory Room, the Throne Room and the Praying Room — strike one's imagination by the fabulous wealth of colours in their decor. The young Tsarevich's apartments with the so-called "Observation Tower" were arranged on the upper floor. It was here that Tsarevich Piotr Alexeyevich, the future Emperor Peter the Great, was grown up (he was born in this palace, too, during the night of 30 May 1672).

One of the most beautiful interiors in the palace, the Throne Room, served as the Sovereign's smaller audience room. Its central window was called a "petitioning" window — a box was pulled down outside of it and everybody could put his or her petition into it. Usually the petitions remained without attention for a long time, so people named this public mailbox "a long-time box", hence a popular Russian expression — to "put off into a long-time box", i.e. to "shelve something".

**The Terem Palace. The Golden (Red) Porch
Decoration in the form of a lion head**

The Terem Palace. Regalia of Tsar Mikhail Romanov

The Terem Palace. The Throne Chamber

43

The Patriarch's Palace and the Church of the Twelve Apostles. 1642–55
Architects: Alexei Korolkov, Ivan Semionov, Davyd Okhlebinin, Taras Timofeyev, Antip Konstantinov

The Ivan the Great Bell-Tower was put up in 1505–08 by the Italian architect Bon Friazin on the site of the Church of St John Climacus that had been erected in 1329 under Ivan Kalita. In 1532 another Italian architect, Petrok the Small, began to attach to "Ivan the Great" a bell-tower for a huge bell weighing some 1000 *poods* (3,600 pounds)⊠ Russian master craftsmen had completed its construction by 1551.

In 1600 a terrible famine broke out in the country and Boris Godunov, who was then on the throne, started a reconstruction of the bell-tower in order to provide people with jobs. The bell-tower was raised to the present-day dimensions (82 m) and its domes were gilded. The lower storey was occupied by the Church of St John Climacus, hence the name – the Ivan the Great Bell-Tower. Later, in the seventeenth century, the so-called Philaretes' annex, which blended well with the ensemble, was put up on the northern side of the bell-tower. Today the bell-tower and belfry have 21 bells.

Complex of the Ivan the Great Bell-Tower. 1505–08, architect: Bon Friazin⊡
1532–43, architect: Petrok the Small⊡ 1600, 1624, architect: Bazhen Ogurtsov

The Patriarch's Palace. The Main Corridor
The veil and staffs of Patriarch Nikon
Second half of the 17th century

In 1653 Patriarch Nikon entrusted to the stone-carver Alexei Korolkov the construction of a palace and the Church of the Twelve Apostles at the Patriarch's Courtyard. In the eastern part the palace had three storeys and a small addition that became the fourth floor, appeared only at the end of the seventeenth century and became known as the Peter Palace – legend has it that Peter the Great concealed himself there during the Streltsy mutiny. The new edifice rivalled the Tsar's palace in luxury and magnificence. It consisted of a home church, dwelling apartments, reception and service rooms. Worthy of special attention is the Cross Chamber — the main reception room of the Russian Patriarchs that struck contemporaries by its huge dimensions and unusual design of the vault resting merely on the walls. Nowadays the palace houses a rich collection of Russian applied art of the seventeenth century.

The Patriarch's Palace. Apartments of Patriarch Nikon

The Patriarch's Palace. The Large Cross (Chrism Preparation) Chamber
The display of the Museum of 17th-Century Russian Applied Art and Everyday Life

The Great Kremlin Palace. 1838–50. Architect: Konstantin Thon

At the very top of Borovitsky Hill soars the majestic building of the Great Kremlin Palace facing the Moskva River. It was constructed in 1838–49 to a project by Academician Konstantin Thon on the site of the eighteenth-century palace designed by Rastrelli that had burnt down in 1812. According to the architect's project this elaborate architectural complex was to unite numerous structures built in different periods. The façade and interiors of the new imperial residence were designed in the Russian style characteristic of the majority of Thon's works. The front of the palace is adorned with pilasters and window surrounds in the style of white-stone Russian architecture of the seventeenth century. The main entrance leads to a marble lobby decorated with columns of Serdobolye granite. The majestic granite staircase leads one to the first floor, to main halls five of which bear the names of the highest Russian order awards.

The Great Kremlin Palace. The St George Hall

The Great Kremlin Palace
The St Andrew Hall. The Emperor's place

The Great Kremlin Palace. The St Andrew Hall

The Great Kremlin Palace. The St Vladimir Hall

The Great Kremlin Palace. The St Catherine Hall

The white and golden St George Hall is named after the Order of St George, the highest award of the Russian Army. Its walls bear marble plaques engraved with the titles of regiments and fleet crews who won this award and more than ten thousand names of the cavaliers of this order. Today the St George Hall is used for various state meetings and receptions. The inauguration of the President of the Russian Federation is also held here.

The name of the St Andrew Hall is associated with the Order of St Andrew the First-Called, the first Russian order introduced by Peter the Great in 1699. The decor of the hall is notable for its mouldings, gilding, semiprecious stones and mirrors. One can see in this interior the three-seat throne produced for the coronation of Nicholas II in 1896.

**The Great Kremlin Palace. The St Catherine Hall
Doors leading to the Main Drawing Room**

The Great Kremlin Palace
The Green Drawing Room. Detail of the interior

"Benefit, honour and glory" – such is the motto of the Order of St Vladimir, Equal to the Apostles, the Grand Prince who gave the name to the next hall. The St Vladimir Hall is the centre of the palatial complex – one can get to the Faceted Chamber, to the Terem Palace and to the St George Hall from it. Provided with two tiers of windows and octagonal in plan, it is surmounted by a dome provided with a lantern.

The design of the Alexander Hall uses the colours of the Order of St Alexander Nevsky. Its walls, faced with artificial pink marble, are decorated with gilding. The dome and the arches have bas-reliefs depicting orders and double-headed eagles.

Simplicity and classical majesty distinguish the St Catherine Hall that formerly served as the Empress's Throne Room. The colours of the order (silvery moiré panels in red frames) harmonize well with the green malachite pilasters and red curtains.

The Great Kremlin Palace. The Peter Hall

The Great Kremlin Palace. The Green Drawing Room

54

The Senate building. 1776–87. Architect: Mikhail Kazakov

In 1776–87 the architect Mikhail Kazakov built by orders of Catherine the Great in the Kremlin a building which housed the Senate, the State Archives, the Treasury and the Noble Assembly. The principal decoration of the Senate became the St Catherine Hall. Inspired by the work of the Italian Renaissance architect Antonio Palladio, the designer created a superb rotund hall with an immense dome, unique for its engineering solution. Legend has it that during the test examination of the building, Kazakov stood at its top for more than half an hour, until the builders eliminated scaffoldings, in order to demonstrate its reliability to his colleagues.

The Senate building. The Catherine Hall

The Senate building. Library of the President of Russia

In the nineteenth century the St Catherine Hall was divided with wooden partitions into a number of separate rooms and later it was altered several times again. In 1993 a decision was taken to give the Senate building its original appearance. From 1996, after the completion of restoration work carried out with the use of up-to-date construction technologies, it houses the Residence of the President of the Russian Federation. The building, in which classical interiors have been carefully re-created, is equipped in keeping with the latest achievements in the field of technology. The working study of the President of the Russian Federation is designed in a simple business style the walls are lined with wooden panels, the white ceiling is decorated with an austere golden ornament. Next to the Study is the President's Large Library. Collected here are the books necessary for work of the head of the state and his personal staff. Countless reference books, dictionaries and books on the history of Russia are arranged in wooden glazed bookcases characteristic of library interiors of the late eighteenth century.

The Senate building. The Winter Garden

The State Armoury is the oldest museum of Moscow. It preserves the unique collections of Russian and West European decorative and applied art. The "Arms Chamber" was established by Grand Duke Vasily III for making battle and parade weapons in 1511. Soon it turned from an arms workshop into a special repository for all sorts of gifts to the Tsars or Patriarchs, including those presented by ambassadors, valuable gold and silver vessels from annexed areas, as well as objects formerly owned by disfavoured princes and boyars. In 1806 the Armoury was converted into a museum and in 1813 its doors were opened for the public at large. In several centuries the collections of the museum grew so much that by the middle of the nineteenth century a question arose about new premises for their keeping. In 1851, by orders of Emperor Nicholas I, Konstantin Thon constructed a two-storey building near the Borovitsky Gate of the Kremlin. Rectangular in plan, with two tiers of windows, it was close in architectural design to the Great Kremlin Palace.

The Armoury. Detail of the display. Arms and armour of the early Russian warrior

The Armoury. 1844–51. Architect: Konstantin Thon

The Armoury. The two-seat throne of the Tsars Ivan and Peter. 1682–84 Workshops of the Moscow Kremlin

Worthy of especial interest among museum exhibits are the regalia of royal power – crowns, orbs, sceptres, staffs and thrones — indispensable attributes of luxurious palatial ceremonies. One of the earliest regalia is the "Monomachus hat" presented, according to a legend, by the Byzantine Emperor Constantine Monomachus to his grandson Vladimir Monomachus, the Prince of Kiev. The "Monomachus crown" is made of gold plaques, decorated with gems, trimmed with sable fur and crowned with a golden cross. Its weight is 689 grammes. The last crowned Tsars were two brothers, Ivan and Piotr Alexeyevich, who came to the throne together as co-rulers in 1682. After Russia had been proclaimed an empire, the ritual of crowning was replaced by coronation. Kept in the Armoury is also the "Kazan Hat" commissioned by Ivan the Terrible for the baptism of the Kazan Tsar Ediger and returned to Moscow after his death. A sumptuous crown was made for the coronation of Anna Ioannovna: more than 2,500 gems were used for its decoration. Elizabeth Petrovna was also wearing this crown, after some alterations, at her coronation ceremony. Catherine the Great commissioned for her coronation a new crown to the court jeweller Jérémie Pauzié. It is embellished with 58 large diamonds and about 5,000 small ones, a large ruby and 75 large pearls.

The Armoury. The two-seat throne of the Tsars Ivan and Peter. Detail

**The Armoury
Regalia of the Tsar's power**

The Armoury. Showcases with examples of West European arms and armour

The Armoury. Showcase with the display of Russian secular dress of the 18th to early 20th century

The Armoury. Carriage. Late 16th century. England

The Armoury. Carriage. Detail of decor

The Armoury preserves a superb collection of costumes of the sixteenth to nineteenth century. Festive garments were produced of expensive fabrics decorated with embroidery, gems and fine lace. Of great interest is the collection of Russian, Eastern and West European arms and armour: elegantly decorated festive shields, sabres, helmets and firearms. Well represented in the collection is applied art of the twelfth to seventeenth centuries: church plate, golden and silver vessels, Gospel books and icons in luxurious mounts. The museum also owns a rare collection of carriages and festive horse attire.

The Armoury. Showcase with examples of West European silver

The Armoury. Diamond badge with a portrait miniature of Peter the Great. Early 18th century

The Armoury. Set of arms. Sword. 1814
Craftsman: Nicolas Noël Bouté
Versailles, France

The Armoury
Easter egg: *For the Tercentenary of the Romanov House*. 1913
Jeweller: Henrik Emmanuel Wigström
C. Fabergé Company, St Petersburg

Fiodor Alexeyev. *Red Square in Moscow*. 1801 ▶

Red Square that lies west of the Kremlin was formed in the sixteenth century on the site of a market. Until the middle of the seventeenth century it had changed its name several times before becoming "Red" (meaning "beautiful"). Red Square has always been the city's main square. It was here that public criers announced the Sovereign's will to the people and sometimes the Tsar himself would speak to his subjects from the Lobnoye Mesto or Execution Place, religious processions from the Kremlin cathedrals were held here on feast days.

Panoramic view of Red Square

After the revolution of 1917 a necropolis was formed near the Kremlin wall where major leaders of the Communist movement were buried. In 1924 Lenin was buried there and in 1930 his body was moved to the stone Mausoleum, which completed the formation of the square. In 1918 a tradition to have festive demonstrations and military parades on Red Square was established. One of the most memorable events was the famous parade in honour of the Victory arranged in June 1945, when two hundred banners of the former German regiments and divisions were thrown to the foot of the Mausoleum.

Red Square. Monument to Kuzma Minin and Dmitry Pozharsky. 1804–18. Sculptor: Ivan Martos

**Red Square. Cathedral of the Intercession of the Virgin
(Cathedral of St Basil the Blessed). 1555–61. Architects: Barma and Postnik**

Cathedral of St Basil the Blessed. Shrine with the holy relics of St Basil the Blessed. Late 17th century

In recent years Red Square has regained its historical appearance that largely suffered during the years of Soviet power. The Kazan Cathedral and the Iberian Chapel demolished in the 1930s have been re-created and the Cathedral of the Intercession of the Holy Virgin has been restored.

This cathedral, generally known as the Cathedral of St Basil the Blessed, was constructed in 1551–61 by orders of Ivan the Terrible as a memorial to victories in the war for the conquer of the Kazan Khanate. The architects Barma and Postnik, invited by the Tsar, conceived to erect eight pillar-shaped churches on one base arranging seven of them around the central church consecrated to the Feast of the Intercession of the Holy Virgin — it was on that day, in October 1552, that Kazan was captured. The cathedral owes its second name to the tenth church erected over the tomb of God's fool, St Basil the Blessed. The foundation, basement and details of the building are executed in white stone and the churches themselves are built of bricks, which lends the cathedral, in combination with its variegated domes, an unusually picturesque appearance. The inner space of the cathedral is not large, so the most solemn services used to be performed in olden times on Red Square.

The cathedral could be destroyed several times. In 1812, leaving Moscow, Napoleon ordered to blow it up together with the Kremlin and only a sudden shower prevented his soldiers from fulfilling his command. In the Bolshevik period they intended again to demolish this magnificent architectural monument, but the decision was cancelled. Nowadays the cathedral has been returned to the Orthodox Church. Among its most remarkable features are the priceless sixteenth-century iconostasis and the circular gallery with its frescoes depicting the Garden of Eden.

Set up in front of the cathedral is the monument to Kuzma Minin and Prince Dmitry Pozharsky who headed the popular militia in 1612. Nearby is the elevated platform called Lobnoye Mesto (literally: the Execution Place). Despite its name, it was never used for execution but served for reading state pronouncements.

Cathedral of St Basil the Blessed
The Inner Gallery

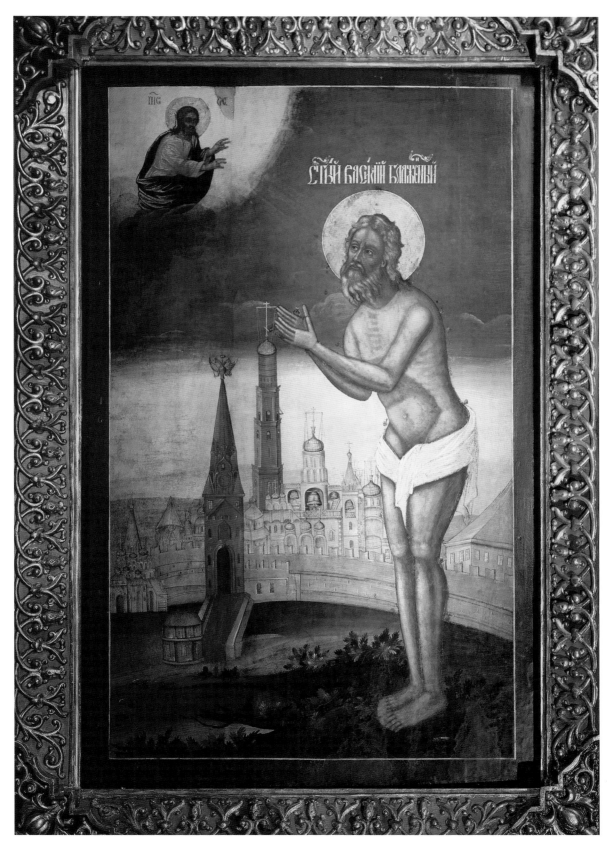

Cathedral of St Basil the Blessed
Icon: *St Basil the Blessed*

Many architectural landmarks emerged on Red Square during more than four centuries of its existence. Despite all their diversity in colour and style, they perfectly accord with the overall space of the square, lending it a rare charm and picturesque quality. One of such notable buildings is the Kazan Cathedral, consecrated to the Icon of Our Lady of Kazan that is believed to have promoted the delivery of Russia from Polish invaders in 1612. Built in 1620–36 with the use of money provided by Prince Dmitry Pozharsky, it became a sort of memorial to killed Russian warriors. Demolished in 1936, the cathedral has been re-created on the former site in 1993.

The eastern side of Red Square was shaped by the Upper Trade Rows put up to a project by the architect Alexander Pomerantsev and the engineer Vladimir Shukhov in 1894. The three-storey building, which consists of the three longitudinal passages, houses more than a thousand shops.

Red Square. The Kazan Cathedral. Second quarter of the 17th century. Re-created in 1993

**Red Square. The Lenin Mausoleum. 1930
Architect: Alexei Shchusev**

Red Square. The Upper Trade Rows (State Department Store). 1889–93
Architect: Alexander Pomerantsev, engineer: Vladimir Shukhov

The structures of iron, glass and concrete harmoniously blend here with the shapes of early Russian architecture. Used in the decor of the fronts are Finnish granite, Tarusa marble and sandstone.

The Iberian Gate (1680) with a gate church consecrated to the Iberian Icon of the Mother of God also contributes to the picturesque appearance of Red Square. Dismantled in 1931, it has been re-created in 1995. Next to the gate is the building of the State Historical Museum closing the perspective of Red Square from the north. According to the concept of Vladimir Sherwood, its designer, the architecture of the museum building was to reflect the ideas of national history. Therefore the architect turned for inspiration to the ancient structures that were to make a single ensemble with it — the Cathedral of St Basil the Blessed and the towers of the Kremlin.

Red Square
The Upper Trade Rows. The central hall

The State Historical Museum. 1874–83
Architects: Vladimir Sherwood, A. Popov; engineer: A. Semionov

The ancient Russian motifs decorating the fronts of the Historical Museum were borrowed from diverse structures dating from the seventeenth century. Despite a touch of eclecticism, the building integrated well with the ensemble of Red Square.

In 1995, to mark the 50th Anniversary of the Victory in the War of 1941–45, an equestrian monument to Marshal Zhukov, an outstanding army commander, created by the sculptor Viacheslav Klykov, was set up in front of the northern façade of the museum overlooking Manège Square.

Monument to Marshal Georgy Zhukov. 1995
Sculptor: Viacheslav Klykov; architect: Yu. Grigoryev

The Iberian (Resurrection) Gate. 1680
Re-created in 1995. Architect: O. Zhurin

View of the Kremlin and Red Square from Manège Square

Alongside the north-western wall of the Kremlin stretches a wide strip of shady parkland decorated with flowerbeds and pieces of sculpture. This is the Alexander Garden, a place of rest favoured by the Muscovites. It was laid out in 1821–23 to a project by the architect Osip Bove on the place of the Neglinnaya River bed by then covered with earth. A magnificent cast-iron railing with a decorative gate (after a drawing by E. Pascal) separates the upper section of the garden from Mokhovaya Street and Manège Square. The pillars of the railing are executed as Roman fascia symbolizing Russia's victory in the Patriotic War of 1812. In May 1967, to celebrate the 22nd Anniversary of the Victory in the War of 1941–45, a new memorial — the Tomb of the Unknown Soldier — was opened in the Alexander Garden. The eternal fire burning near it has been brought from the heroic city of Leningrad.

Railing of the Alexander Garden. After a drawing by E. Pascal

Tomb of the Unknown Soldier near the Kremlin wall

Manège Square ▶

**Interior of the Okhotny Riad Trade Centre
on Manège Square**

**Manège Square
in night illumination**

At the northern side Red Square adjoins Manège Square , one of the oldest in the capital of Russia, that took shape in 1485–95. After the construction of the Kremlin walls had been ended, a decision was taken to remove all wooden structures near the Kremlin so as to save it from possible conflagrations. In 1817 the building of the Manège was erected in the centre of the square, hence its name. Put up to a project by Augustin de Béthencourt in the neo-Classical style, it had no analogues in the architecture of those days. A vast space with an area of 7,425 square metres is covered by a single roof lying without and intermediate supports on wooden rafters each 45 metres long. In 2005 the Manège building badly suffered from fire, but it has been quickly restored to its former appearance and today graces the square again.

Vasily Polenov. *A Moscow Courtyard*. 1878 ▶

The radius-and-ring scheme of Moscow began to form as early as the thirteenth and fourteenth centuries. It was then that the Great Settlement took shape around the Kremlin. Later the fortified Kitai-Gorod was established on its site. With an increase of the city's population, it grew over its former boundaries several times. Thus the White Town appeared, with its boundaries by the Boulevard Ring; then the Wooden Town emerged, etc. Roads connecting the capital with various regions of the country diverged in different directions from the Kremlin. The Ordynskaya Road, which served mainly to supply Moscow with the grain, led to the south-east; the Vladimir Road to the east, the Dmitrov Road to the north, the Tver Road to the north-west and the Smolensk Road to the west. Today the central streets of the capital — Ordynka, Varvarka (on the site of the former Vladimir Road), Bolshaya and Malaya Dmitrovka, Tverskaya and Arbat Streets — are lying along these old radial directions. The monasteries, built at the city's boundaries, were not only centres of spiritual, religious and cultural life, but, what was essential, played the role of powerful outposts defending approaches to Moscow.

Varvarka Street. In the forefront, the Church of St George-on-Pskov-Hill. 1657–58

Varvarka Street. The Chambers of the English Courtyard. 15th–17th century

One of the most beautiful architectural complexes of Moscow, Theatre Square, was created in 1821–24 to a project by the architect Osip Bove. After the end of the War of 1812 it was necessary to restore Moscow that had burnt down during Napoleon's invasion. Bove was put at the head of the Building Commission created for that purpose in 1813. According to his plan the entire centre of the city, including Theatre Square, with the Bolshoi Theatre dominating it, was to gain a new appearance. In 1853 the building of the theatre was completely devastated by fire and in 1856 it was re-created to a project by the architect Albert Cavos, who designed its fronts in the neo-Classical style. The Bolshoi Theatre, the country's largest musical stage, was founded in 1776 and since then its glory has gone far beyond the borders of Russia. Among those who performed on its stage in different periods were the outstanding singers and dancers Fiodor Chaliapin, Antonina Nezhdanova, Leonid Sobinov, Ivan Kozlovsky, Sergei Lemeshev, Galina Ulanova, Maya Plisetskaya and Maris Liepa.

Overlooking Theatre Square are also the Maly Art Theatre, Russia's earliest drama theatre, and the Metropol Hotel designed in the Art Nouveau style.

The State Bolshoi Theatre. 1825, architect: Osip Bove; 1856, architect: Albert Cavos

Theatre Square and the building of the Metropol Hotel. 1899–1903. Architect: William Walcott

Tverskaya Square. Building of the Moscow Government
Built to a project by Mikhail Kazakov. 1945, architects: D. Chechulin, M. Posokhin, A. Mdoyants

From Manege Square starts the principal street of Moscow — Tverskaya Street. One of the city's radial thoroughfares, it was formed in the fourteenth century thanks to its closer relations with the north-western principalities, primarily with Tver and Novgorod the Great. Moscow used to begin with Tverskaya Street for many travellers. It was considered prestigious to dwell on this street, although old aristocratic families preferred more quiet places — Povarskaya, Pokrovka, Ostozhenka and Volkhonka Streets.

After the October Revolution Tverskaya Street was renamed and until 1990s was known as Gorky Street. In 1935 this ancient street has nearly completely lost its historical appearance as a result of large-scale reconstruction of the city's centre under the supervision of the eminent Soviet architect Arkady Mordvinov. Like some other streets in the city, it was widened by means of shifting and partly demolishing old buildings and then replacing them with new, more gorgeous ones.

Not far from its beginning Tverskaya Street comes to the square of the same name designed at the end of the eighteenth century by the architect Mikhail Kazakov. In the centre of the square, opposite the Government Building (the former residence of the Moscow Governor General) stands the monument to the founder of Moscow, Prince Yury Dolgoruky, unveiled in 1948, when Moscow celebrated the 800th anniversary of its foundation.

Tverskaya Square. Monument to Prince Yury Dolgoruky. 1954.
Sculptors: S. Orlov, A. Antropov, N. Shtamm; architect: V. Andreyev

Tverskaya Street. Building of the former English Club. 1780
Restored after 1812. Architect: Adam Menelaws

Among the few surviving eighteenth and nineteenth structures on Tverskaya Street one's attention is attracted by an Empire-style building separated from the thoroughfare by an elegant railing with lions. This former estate of Count Razumovsky was erected in 1780 and rebuilt in 1812 by Adam Menelaws. Until 1917 the building housed the fashionable English Club that was converted into the Museum of the Revolution in 1924.

Changing its appearance in the course of history, Tverskaya Street always remained the main street of Moscow, retaining its main quality — an imposing, representative character. Wide and majestic, it still remains today one of the most busy streets in the city. It is here that the most fashionable and expensive shopping centres, including the famous Yeliseyev Food Shop, founded in the late nineteenth century, are situated.

Tverskaya Street. The Yeliseyev Food Shop. Selling area

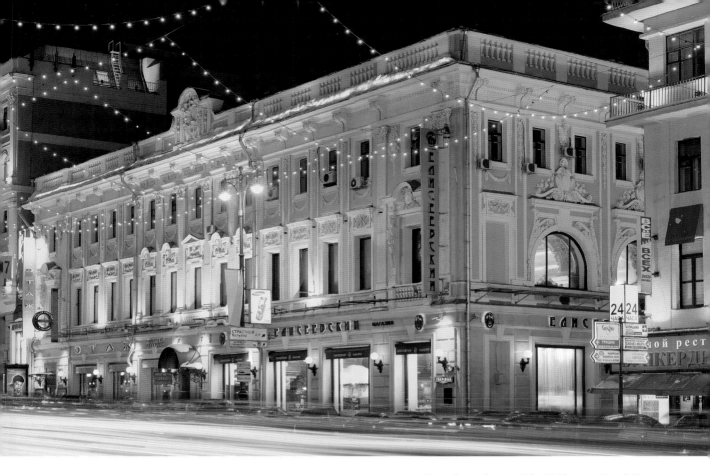

Tverskaya Street. The Yeliseyev Food Shop

Tverskaya Street. The National Hotel. 1903
Architect: Alexander Ivanov

Tverskaya Street by night

Building of the Moscow Arts Academic Theatre named after Maxim Gorky. 1902. Architect: Fiodor Shekhtel

Tverskaya Street is closely associated in the Muscovites' memory with Alexander Pushkin. It was not far from here, in the Goncharov mansion owned by an aristocratic Moscow family, that a romantic story of the poet's love to their daughter Natalie unfolded, as the fountain recently installed near the Nikitskiye Gate reminds us today.

Tverskaya Street might well be called "Theatre Street". Every night thousands of the Muscovites and guests of the capital arrive here so as to enjoy the performance of their favourite actors. The Maly Art Theatre, the Yermolova Theatre, the Satire Theatre, the Operetta Theatre and the Great Puppy Theatre — this is a list, even not a complete one, of the theatres located on Tverskaya and adjoining streets.

Tverskaya Street is especially good on festive days, when traffic is suspended on it and the entire space is given for popular entertainment according to the old, recently revived tradition. The street becomes unusual, fantastically beautiful by night, when thousands of illumination fires flood it.

Tverskoi Boulevard
Fountain-rotonda *Natalie and Alexander*. **1999**
Sculptor: M. Dronov;
architects: M. Belov and M. Kharitonov

Malaya Nikitskaya Street. N. Riabushinsky's Mansion. 1900
Architect: Fiodor Shekhtel

N. Igumnov's Mansion on Bolshaya Yakimanka Street. 1889–93

The vividly jagged line of façades and a great stylistic variety of structures are characteristic features of Moscow streets. Classicism and neo-Gothic can be seen here neighbouring Art Nouveau, Constructivism and the Stalin Empire of the 1930s– 1950s, or sometimes elaborate ancient patterns of seventeenth-century buildings.

A special place among Moscow streets belongs to the Boulevard and Garden Rings, which emerged on the site of the removed defensive structures the traces of which can be seen to this day on Gogol Boulevard. In the nineteenth century the Moscow aristocracy used to settle at the Boulevard Ring: they built here rich mansions and large social buildings, planted limes, decorative shrubs and flowers. The Boulevard Ring still is one of the most favourite areas in Moscow with its very special atmosphere. The Garden Ring is absolutely different from the Boulevard Ring. In the nineteenth century wide boulevards— Zubov, Smolensk and Novinsky Boulevards — were also created here, but later trees were removed to enlarge a traffic capacity and as a result the Garden Ring has become an exclusively transport thoroughfare.

**Bolshaya Nikitskaya Street. In the forefront,
the Moscow School of Political Research. 18th century**

Arbat Street ▶

**Arbat Street. The Central House of Actors
Detail of the façade**

Arbat, one of the oldest streets in Moscow, lies on the ancient Smolensk Road. In early times craftsmen used to settle in this area, which is reflected in the names of the surrounding lanes: Silver Lane, Carpenter Lane, etc. In the eighteenth century Arbat Street became an aristocratic region; later prominent members of the merchant class began to oust the hereditary nobility. In the course of its history the street burnt down several times and was built anew, so buildings of the nineteenth and twentieth centuries prevail here today. Before the 1960s one could go by a tram along Arbat Street, then a trolley-bus service replaced trams and still later it has become the first historical pedestrian zone in Moscow.

**Arbat Street. Sculpture-fountain *Princess Turandot*
at the entrance to the Vakhtangov Theatre. 1996
Sculptor: A. Burganov**

**Arbat Street. The Central House of Actors. 1913–14
Architect: V. Dubovsky, N. Arkhipov**

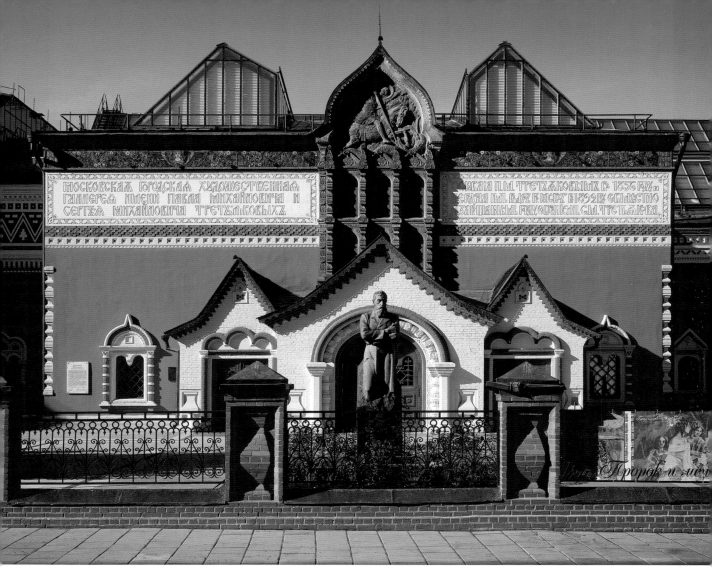

The State Tretyakov Gallery. Main façade. 1902–04
Designed by Victor Vasnetsov

In the area behind the Moskva River, on the ancient Lavrushinsky Lane, is situated a museum, which preserves one of the world's most famous collections of Russian painting — the State Tretyakov Gallery. It was founded in 1874 by Pavel Tretyakov, a well-known merchant and patron of art. The present-day building of the gallery, the façade of which was designed in the ancient Russian style by the artist Victor Vasnetsov in 1902–04, united several structures put up in different periods and housing Tretyakov's collection in different years. In 1892 this patron of art presented his gallery to the city of Moscow remaining its custodian to the end of his life.

Today's Tretyakov Gallery is both a huge museum and a major scientific centre. Its collections amount to more than 100,000 exhibits. The department of early Russian painting contains superb icons of the twelfth to eighteenth century, including works by Andrei Rublev, Dionysius and Simon Ushakov. Some of them were recently transferred to the nearby Church of Nicholas at Tolmachi, the parishioners of which now have a possibility to pray in front of these ancient sacred objects.

Andrei Rublev. *Ca* 1360/1370–1430s. **Icon:** *The Old Testament Trinity.* 1410s

Alexander Ivanov. 1806–1858. *The Appearance of Christ to the People.* **1837–57**

Mikhail Vrubel. 1856–1910. *The Demon.* **1890**

Vasily Perov. 1834–1882. *Troika.* **1866**

The Tretyakov Gallery possesses a very rich collection of Russian painting of the eighteenth to early twentieth century. Displayed in its rooms are canvases by the major Russian painters — Alexander Ivanov, Vasily Tropinin, Alexei Venetsianov, Ivan Aivazovsky, Ivan Shishkin, Vasily Perov, Vasily Surikov, Ilya Repin, Mikhail Vrubel, Valentin Serov and many others. The works created in the post-revolutionary period, from 1917 top the present time, can be seen in the building on Krymsky Val Street, also a branch of the Tretyakov Gallery.

Valentin Serov. 1865–1911
Girl with Peaches
Portrait of Vera Mamontova. **1887**

Today's Moscow is not only the capital of the Russian Federation, but the centre of the Russian Orthodox religion as well. Worthy of special interest among two hundred churches functioning in it is the Cathedral of the Theophany at Yelokhovo. Built at the turn of the eighteenth and nineteenth centuries, it has never interrupted its religious activities. It is also famous for the fact that the future great Russian poet, Alexander Pushkin, was baptized here in 1799.

Church of the Theophany at Yelokhovo. 1837–45
Architect: Yefgraf Tiurin

Church of St Nicholas at Pyzhy
Late 17th century

Panoramic view of Moscow ▶

Cathedral of the Redeemer. Detail of the façade

The Cathedral of the Redeemer, one of the most celebrated Moscow churches, was conceived by Emperor Alexander I in gratitude to God for the protection of Russia from Napoleon's onslaught in 1812. Originally it was supposed to build the cathedral on the Sparrow Hills to a project by Alexander Vitberg, but owing to specific geological features of the terrain the project was cancelled. After the death of Alexander I it was his successor, Nicholas I, who chose an architect for the cathedral and a site for its construction. He entrusted the building of the cathedral on the bank of the Moskva River to Konstantin Thon. The work lasted for 44 years and in 1883 the cathedral was consecrated in a majestic atmosphere.

Cathedral of the Redeemer. Designed by the architect Konstantin Thon. Re-created in the 1990s

View of the Cathedral of the Redeemer from the side of the Patriarch's Bridge

Cathedral of the Redeemer. Detail of wall painting

Cathedral of the Redeemer. Interior

**Monument to Peter the Great. 1997
Sculptor: Zurab Tsereteli**

The five domes of the cross-in-plan cathedral attain the height of 103 metres. Originally encircling the building at the level of the basement floor was a gallery containing the first museum of the War of 1812. All the battles, the units that distinguished themselves and their commanders, the names of the perished and awarded officers were recorded on white marble panels. The fronts of the edifice were adorned with high reliefs executed by Alexander Loganovsky, Nikolai Ramazanov and Peter Klodt. The outstanding artists of the period — Piotr Basin, Henryk Siemiradzki, Vasily Surikov, Konstantin Makovsky and others — toiled for twenty-three years on the painted decor of the cathedral. A tent-shaped chancel canopy executed according to a special commission replaced the traditional iconostasis.

In 1931 the Cathedral of the Redeemer was exploded and its decor, except for some high reliefs, disappeared without a trace. It was supposed to erect on the site of the cathedral a giant Palace of the Soviets, but the outbreak of war in 1941 prevented from realizing this plan. In 1960 an outdoor swimming pool "Moskva" was created on the area of the destroyed cathedral. The re-creation of the cathedral to its original appearance and on the historical site began with the foundation of a chapel in honour of the Icon of the Mother of God "Derzhavnaya" on 5 December 1990. This icon, discovered in the village of Kolomenskoye on the day of Nicholas II's abdication, proved to be Russia's support and protection. The construction of the cathedral itself began with the blessing of the Patriarch of Moscow and all the Russias in 1994; in 2000 Moscow's sacred object adorned the picturesque banks of the Moskva River again.

The principal water artery, the Moskva River has long since played an important role in the life of the city. In the Soviet period, thanks to the construction of an elaborate system of sluices and the deep Moscow Canal that linked it with the Upper Volga, the Moskva River turned into one of principal trade ways of the region.

View of the Moskva River from the observation deck of the Cathedral of the Redeemer

Chapel of the Icon of the Mother of God "Derzhavnaya" near the Cathedral of the Redeemer

The blocks of buildings situated alongside the banks of the Moskva River near the Cathedral of the Redeemer are endowed with a special charm. Old churches, large and small mansions, urban estates of different ages and styles preserve the unique atmosphere of old, pre-revolutionary Moscow. The construction boom of the turn of the nineteenth and twentieth centuries, when Art Nouveau was especially popular, also touched these places. One of the most prominent examples of this architecture became the tenement house of the engineer Piotr Pertsov built to sketches by the artist Sergei Maliutin with the use of motifs borrowed from early Russian architecture — high pitched roofs and polychrome tile insets. In 1908–12 the basement of this building housed the famous artistic cabaret "The Bat".

Church of the Holy Trinity at Bersenevo. 1654

The former P. Pertsov's tenement house 1906–10. Architect: N. Zhukov After drawings by Sergei Maliutin

The idea to create a large museum of arts in Moscow arose as early as the nineteenth century. The city's Duma allotted for this purpose a plot of land not far from the Kremlin — the territory of the former Carriage Court. A competition was declared for the best project of a museum building and its official name was approved — the Alexander III Museum of Fine Arts. Nineteen architects took part in the competition won by Roman Klein, who was awarded the Gold Medal. Klein was entrusted to develop the final version of the project and to carry out its construction.

The Pushkin Museum of Fine Arts
Art of Ancient Rome

The Pushkin Museum of Fine Arts. 1898–1912.
Roman Klein, sculptor: Hugo Zaleman

The Pushkin Museum of Fine Arts. Italian courtyard

Rembrandt. 1606–1669
Portrait of an Elderly Woman. 1854

The ceremony of the foundation of the Museum of Fine Arts took place on 17 August 1898 in the presence of Emperor Nicholas II. In 1904 the construction of the building was finished and on 31 May 1912 the museum welcomed its first visitors.

The building is designed in the neo-Classical style, as an ancient temple with an Ionic colonnade. The interiors are decorated according to the traditions of the ages reflected in the exhibitions. A large role in the development of the programme of the museum and the organization of its work belonged to Professor Ivan Tsvetayev, Doctor of Literature and the History of Art, who became its first Director.

The Pushkin Museum of Fine Arts
Art of the Italian Renaissance

Paul Gauguin. *The Queen (The King's Wife).* **1896**

The collection of the Museum of Fine Arts has been based on the assemlage of the Cabinet of Fine Arts and Antiquities of Moscow University. It consisted of plaster casts of ancient statues, dummies, painted and galvanoplasitc copies representing the basic phases in the evolution of world art from antiquity to the new times. A valuable acquisition was the collection of Egyptian papyri that had belonged to the Russian Egyptologist Vladimir Golenishchev and was bought from him by the state as a gift for the museum. The rooms of Italian art were embellished with authentic works of Italian painting and objects of applied and decorative art of the thirteenth to fifteenth century from the collection of Mikhail Shchepkin. In the 1920s and 1930s the museum collections were substantially enlarged by objects from nationalized estates of the nobility, from the Historical Museum, the museums of the Kremlin and the Tretyakov Gallery.

Auguste Renoir. 1841–1919. *Nude.* **1876**

Vincent van Gogh. 1853–1890. *Red Vineyards at Arles.* **1888**

Many canvases by West European masters were handed over to the museum from the State Hermitage and the Leningrad Museum Reserve. In the 1940s exhibits from the disbanded Museum of New Western Art, created on the basis of the collections of two Russian patrons of art, Sergei Shchukin and Ivan Morozov, who collected mainly European paintings. This allowed the museum to form one of the world's best collections of French painting of the late nineteenth and early twentieth centuries. At the present time the stocks of the Pushkin Museum of Fine Arts (as it has began to be called since 1932) number more than 2,000,000 works of painting, graphic art, sculpture and applied art. The pride of the collection are canvases by Rembrandt, Pieter Paul Rubens, Anthonis van Dyck, Nicolas Poussin and, naturally, paintings by the French Impressionists and Post-Impressionists: Claude Monet, Auguste Renoir, Paul Gauguin, Vincent van Gogh, Pablo Picasso, Henri Matisse and other fine artists.

In 1985, the new Museum of Private Collections, initiated by the well-known art collector, Doctor of Arts Ilya Zilberstein, began to function as a scientific department of the museum. The core of its displays was formed of private collections exhibited in a separate building — the former wing of the Princes Golitsyn located near the museum.

Tsvetnoi Boulevard. Fountain near the Moscow Circus building

The Moscow Circus on Tsvetnoi Boulevard is one of the oldest in the country. The building housing it was constructed in 1880 for the Circus of Albert Salamonsky that became the first state circus after the revolution. The glory of the Moscow Circus in Russia and abroad was largely due to its famous clowns — Caran-d'Ache, Oleg Popov, Leonid Yengibarov, Mikhail Shuidin and, naturally, Yury Nikulin, who headed it for many years.

Tsvetnoi Boulevard. Sculpture: *Yury Nikulin*. **2000**
Sculptor: A. Rukavishnikov

The Moscow Circus on Tsvetnoi Boulevard. 1880; 1980s (reconstruction)

A special place in the architectural and historical appearance of Moscow oc-
cupy fortified monasteries, which were built in early times on the city's outskirts
to defend approaches to it. One of them, the Novodevichy Convent (New Convent of the Virgin) that protected the city from the south-west, was founded in
1524 by Grand Duke Vasily III in honour of the annexation of Smolensk that
had been a part of the Great Lithuanian Principality since the beginning of the
fifteenth century. In honour of this event the convent was consecrated to Our
Lady of Smolensk. However, as it was the only female cloister among the fortified
monasteries in the environs of Moscow, it became generally known as the New

MOSCOW MONASTERIES AND CONVENTS

The Novodevichy Convent. Founded in 1524

Maiden Convent. The convent was guarded not by nuns, but by male warriors who, for instance, repulsed the Crimean Khan's attack in 1591. The Novodevichy Convent witnessed many dramatic historic events. In 1598, after the death of Tsar Fiodor Ioannovich, his widow Irina took the veil and retired to the Novodevichy Convent where her brother Boris Godunov joined her. It was here, in the convent, that he was elected to the Russian throne. It was also in this convent that Peter the Great confined his disfavoured stepsister, Tsarevna Sophia, and later his first wife, Yevdokia Lopukhina.

**The Novodevichy Convent. In the forefront,
the Church of the Dormition of the Virgin with a refectory (1685–87)**

The ensemble of the Novodevichy Convent includes six churches, the main of which is consecrated to the Smolensk Icon of Our Lady of Smolensk honoured as the most sacred object of the convent. This object, one of the most honoured miraculous icons, is traditionally associated with the Evangelist Luke who painted the image of the Virgin during her life. Worthy of attention are the wonderful murals of the cathedral, executed in the sixteenth and seventeenth centuries, as is the carved iconostasis of seventeenth century. No less superb than the cathedral are also the five-tiered Intercession Bell-Tower, built in 1688 and the Gate Church of the Transfiguration, a fine example of the Russian Baroque. The convent is encircled with a strikingly picturesque fortress wall punctuated by twelve towers built in brick and adorned with white-stone decor.

**The Novodevichy Convent
Church of the Icon of Our Lady of Smolensk. 1524–25
Architect: Aleviz Friazin**

The Donskoi Monastery. Cathedral of the Icon of Our Lady of the Don. 1684–98

The Donskoi Monastery that protected the capital from the south was founded in 1591 by Tsar Fiodor Ioannovich in memory of the miraculous delivery of Moscow from the onslaught of the Crimean Khan Kazy-Girey. The Muscovites won a victory over the Khan's army thanks to the protection of the Icon of Our Lady of the Don, to which the monastery was consecrated. Closed in the Soviet period, the monastery was given back to the Moscow Patriarchy in 1990 and monastic life has resumed in it.

The Donskoi Monastery. Founded in 1591. The bell-tower over the western gate. 1730–32, architect: Domenico Trezzini; 1742–55, architects: A. Yevlashev, D. Ukhtomsky

**Monument to Andrei Rublev in front
of the gate of the Andronikov Monastery
Sculptor: Oleg Komov**

The Andronikov Monastery of the Saviour was the last in the chain of monasteries protecting approaches to Moscow from the south. It was founded in 1359 on the bank of the Yauza River in memory of the miraculous rescue of the Moscow Metropolitan Alexis in a fierce storm at the Black Sea on the way to Constantinople. The monastery owed its name to the first hegumen, Andronicus, a pupil of St Sergius of Radonezh. The white-stone Cathedral of the Saviour in the Andronikov Monastery is one of the earliest architectural monuments of Moscow outside the Kremlin — it was erected between 1425 and 1427. Contemporaries admired the beauty of this cathedral and especially its frescoes created by the celebrated Russian icon-painters Andrei Rublev and Daniel Chorny. Unfortunately the original painting of the cathedral has survived only in the form of some separate fragments. Nevertheless the cathedral strikes us even today by its harmonious appearance, in which majestic monumentality combines with subtle decorativeness. It was in the architecture of this church that the special Moscow style appeared for the first time. Not far from the cathedral stands the Refectory — a massive building of concise forms with powerful walls and simple decor, built in 1504. Its architecture gives us an idea how the stone chambers built in Moscow at the turn of the fifteenth and sixteenth centuries looked like. Next to the Refectory stands the brick Church of the Archangel Michael (1694) that served as a burial place of the Lopukhin boyar family, relations of the first wife of Peter the Great. At the present time the cathedral houses the Andrei Rublev Museum of Early Russian Art. Here one can also see the tomb of the great Russian painter, who spent in the monastery his last years.

**The Andronikov Monastery
Cathedral of the Saviour. 1410–27**

In olden times there were numerous ancient estates of the nobility and several royal residences around Moscow. Over the time many of them entered the territory of the city and former suburban manors were converted into museums of architecture, interior and everyday life. A special place among these complexes belongs to Kolomenskoye, which served as the estate of the grand princes of Moscow from the fourteenth century. It was here that Tsarina Natalia Kirillovna hid with the small Tsareviches, Ivan and Piotr, during the mutiny of the Streltsy in 1682. It was also

OLD MOSCOW COUNTRY ESTATES

N. Podkliuchnikov. *View of Ostankino.* **1856**

from this place that Peter the Great entered Moscow in a majestic atmosphere in 1709, after the victory over the Swedes at Poltava. His daughter, the future Empress Elizabeth Petrovna, was also born here.

The Church of the Ascension at Kolomenskoye, built by Tsar Basil III in honour of the birth of his son, the future Tsar Ivan the Terrible, is regarded as one of the best examples of tent-shaped architecture of the sixteenth century. It is set up on the high bank of the Moskva River that had then afforded a fine view of floodplains and forests.

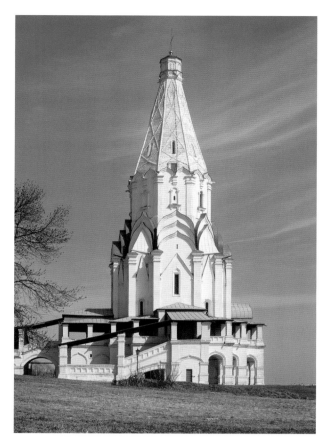

Kolomenskoye. Church of the Ascension. 1532

The slender Church of the Ascension, soaring upwards and decorated with thin pilasters, has the form of a cross with equal ends in plan and is crowned with a tall octagonal tent-shaped top. A covered gallery resting on an arcade, to which lead three porches, skirts the church around the bottom. At the gallery stands a stone throne, from which, according to a legend, the Moscow Sovereign liked to watch falcon hunting.

The Kolomenskoye complex includes today, in addition to the Church of the Ascension, the Church and Bell-Tower of St George, the Church of the Icon of Our Lady of Kazan and the Water Supply Tower. In 1930–59 Kolomenskoye was a museum of early Russian architecture and for this purpose remarkable examples of Russian wooden architecture were brought to this area.

**Kolomenskoye. The Tsar's Courtyard
The House of Peter the Great. 1702
Brought from Arkhangelsk**

Kolomenskoye. Church of the Icon of Our Lady of Kazan. 1649–50

Tsaritsyno. The Grain House and the Gallery-Railing with a gate. 1784–85. Architect: Vasily Bazhenov

Located at the south-east of Moscow, the Tsaritsyno estate belonged to Tsarina Irina, Boris Godunov's sister, and was then known as Bogorodskoye. Later Peter the Great presented it to the Moldavian ruler Dmitry Kantemir. In 1775 Catherine the Great bought the land of the estate and called it Tsaritsyno Selo (Tsarina's Village). Tsaritsyno is the place associated with the great eighteenth-century Russian architect Vasily Bazhenov. It was to Bazhenov, elected to three Academies, that the Empress entrusted the construction of a small romantic palace and park complex, which was to become a sort of memorial to the victory in the Russo-Turkish War of 1768–74. The main condition was to create a whole ensemble of buildings in the then fashionable Gothic style.

Tsaritsyno. Figured bridge. 1776–78
Architect: Vasily Bazhenov

**Tsaritsyno. The Figured (Vine Grape) Gate. 1777–78
Architect: Vasily Bazhenov**

The construction of Tsaritsyno, the "Versailles in the environs of Moscow", started in 1776. By the arrival of the Empress in 1785 had been erected the palace, the Opera House, the Cavaliers Blocks, the Gate and the Grain House — one of the largest buildings with kitchens, confectionaries, various cellars and dwellings for servants. The bridges adorned with white-marble ornaments made the complex especially picturesque. Catherine, however, did not like the palace built by Bazhenov and ordered to dismantle it. In 1786–93 Mikhail Kazakov was building the so-called Great Palace on its site, but did not complete the project. From the late 1970s restoration work is under way at Tsaritsyno. At the present time many monuments have already been restored in keeping with Bazhenov's original concept.

**The Large Bridge across a ravine. 1778, 1784–85
Architect: Vasily Bazhenov**

**Ostankino. The Palace. 1792–98. Architects: Francesco Camporesi,
Pavel Argunov, A. Mironov and others**

The quiet tenor of life in Moscow, remote from the bustle of the capital city of St Petersburg, pleased many rich aristocrats. There are several estates within the precincts of present-day Moscow that had belonged to once most prominent members of the Tsar's entourage. In the 1790s the well-known patron of arts, Count Nikolai Sheremetev, began to construct a palace-theatre on his estate Ostankino in the neighbourhood of Moscow. Designed according to the classical canons, at the first glance the structure seems to have been built in brick, although the basic material employed for its construction was timber, with vertically set up logs. Many Russian and foreign architects contributed to this project, but its main creators were Russian serf craftsmen, who worked under the supervision of the architect Pavel Argunov, a serf of Count Sheremetev. And the interiors created by them amaze us no less today by their subtle taste and mastery of execution. At the present time Ostankino functions as a museum of Russian decorative and applied art of the eighteenth and nineteenth centuries.

**Ostankino. The passage gallery
to the Italian Pavilion. Detail**

The main building of State Moscow University on Sparrow Hills. 1949–53
Architects: Lev Rudnev, P. Abrosimov, A. Khriakov

After the revolution of 1917 old patriarchal Moscow sharply began to change its appearance. In the 1920s and 1930s a whole series of edifices in the Constructivist style was erected, including the Planetarium on Sadovaya-Kudrinskaya Square, the Krasnopresnensky Department Store and the Newspaper Izvestiya building. By the middle of the 1930s a traditional trend gained the upper hand in architecture, which greatly influenced the appearance of Moscow. It acquired a solemn look, befitting the capital, but in the process many old buildings were sacrificed in favour of new construction projects; they were mercilessly destroyed despite their historical and artistic value. In 1947, to mark the 800th Anniversary of the city, a plan for the construction of seven high-rise buildings was approved. Erected within the subsequent decade, the buildings of the University on Lenin (Sparrow) Hills, the Ministry of Foreign Affairs, the Ministry of Railway Communications, the Ukraine Hotel and the dwelling houses on the Kotelnicheskaya Embankment and near the Red Gate made up a sort of architectural ensemble that became a notable feature of Moscow's skyline.

The Ukraine Hotel. 1956
Architects: A. Mordvinov, V. Oltarzhevsky, V. Kalish

The Revolution Square Metro Station. 1938
Architect: A. Dushkin

The first Metro line in Russia that began to function in Moscow in 1935 has recently celebrated its 70th anniversary. The Kurskaya, Komsomolskaya, Revolution Square and other stations, designed in the 1930s–1950s by the country's best architects, are regarded now as architectural monuments. The name of "underground palaces" of Moscow befits these magnificent architectural structures decorated with a truly fabulous luxury. Used for their construction were various kinds of marble, granite, semiprecious stones, bronze, coloured glass and mosaics. Major Soviet masters decorated the metro stations and overground vestibules with paintings, pieces of sculpture, richly coloured stained glass windows and sumptuous mouldings. Today the Moscow Metro has twelve lines with an overall length of 275.6 kilometres and numbers 170 stations.

The Revolution Square Metro Station
Detail of decor

The Komsomolskaya-Radialnaya Metro Station
Majolica panel: *Metro Builders*. 1935
Artist: Yevgeny Lanceray

The Komsomolskaya-Koltsevaya Metro Station. 1952
Architects: Alexei Shchusev, V. Kakorin,
A. Zabolotskaya

Moscow has many green boulevards, parks and gardens, where its residents like to spend their spare time. Worthy of special mention among them is the All-Russian Exhibition Centre. Here, amidst the verdure of a huge park stretching for more than 200 hectares, in 82 pavilions with a general area of more than 200,000 square metres, permanently function various industrial and trade exhibitions and fairs are organized. The original project of the complex was created in 1937 by the architect V. Oltarzhevsky, who based it on the compositional solution First All-Russian Exhibition of Agriculture and Handicrafts held in 1923. In 1939–41 the territory was occupied by the All-Union Agricultural Exhibition and from 1959 to 1992 it was known as the Exhibition of the Achievements of People's Economy. Major architects of the country participated in the creation of this complex, the focus of which became the central pavilion built in 1954 to a project by Vladimir Shchuko and Ye. Stoliarov. One of entrances to the exhibition is decorated with the immense sculptural group *The Worker and the Collective-Farm Woman* created by Vera Mukhina. Installed in 1939, it has become a symbol of new Moscow.

The All-Russian Exhibition Centre. Fountain: *Friendship of Peoples*. **1953**
Architect: K. Topuridze; sculptor: D. Konstantinovsky

The All-Russian Exhibition Centre

**Victory Square. The Triumphal Arch
Designed by Osip Bove. Re-created in 1966**

In 1995, to commemorate the 50th Anniversary of the Victory in the War of 1941–45, the Victory Memorial was unveiled on Poklonnaya Hill in Moscow. It became a sort of supplement to the memorial complex devoted to the War of 1812 that had existed there since the 1960s. All the elements of the Memorial, created to a project by the sculptor Zurab Tsereteli — the Years of War Avenue, Victors' Square and the Victors' Obelisk — glorify in a symbolic form the Victory of 1945. The complex also includes the Museum of the Great Patriotic War and places of worship of three different confessions — the Orthodox Church of St George, a mosque and a synagogue.

**The Victory Memorial
Church of St George. 1993–95
Architect: A. Poliansky**

**Memorial in honour of the Victory in the Great Patriotic War of 1941–45 on Poklonnaya Hill. 1983–95
Architects: A. Poliansky, V. Budayev, L. Vavakin; sculptor: Zurab Tsereteli**

Bridge near the Kiev Railway Station. 2002
Architect: Yury Platonov

Nautilus Trade Complex on Nikolskaya Street. 2004

The "Tower-2000" with the "Bagration" Footbridge. 2000. Architect: Yury Platonov

On the road to Yaroslavl, some 60 kilometres from Moscow, lies one of the principal Russian Orthodox sacred places — the Trinity-St Sergius Monastery founded in the middle of the fourteenth century by St Sergius of Radonezh. Retreating from the world after the death of his relatives, Sergius and his brother settled in a wooded locality, on Makovets Hill, not far from the town of Radonezh. Soon a small hermitage consecrated to the Holy and Life-Giving Trinity was established. The first wooden Church of the Holy Trinity was consecrated in the 1340s. It was in this period that the first rule of cenobitic monasticism was adopted in the

THE TRINITY-ST SERGIUS MONASTERY

The Trinity-St Sergius Monastery. Founded in 1337

brotherhood of St Sergius and he was elected its hegumen. Thanks to the authority of St Sergius and his deeds of devotion the Trinity Monastery rapidly grew into Russia's spiritual centre. Prince Dmitry Donskoi had come here before the crucial Battle of Kulikovo to ask a blessing from Sergius. Later the Trinity-St Sergius Monastery continued to grow and strengthen and by 1917 it had been the largest monastery in Russia. In 1920 it was closed, but in 1947 returned to the Russian Orthodox Church and monastic life there has resumed.

The Trinity-St Sergius Monastery. Refectory with the Church of St Sergius of Radonezh. 1686–92

The complex of the Trinity-St Sergius Monastery, formed between the fifteenth and nineteenth centuries, includes many outstanding monuments of Russian architecture. The earliest of them is the Cathedral of the Holy Trinity (1422–23), which contains a sanctuary with the holy relics of St Sergius. The cathedral was constructed on the site of the earliest wooden church built of logs by the founder of the monastery. Around it are situated the Church of the Descent of the Holy Spirit, the Cathedral of the Dormition, a refectory with the Church of St Sergius of Radonezh, the Churches of SS Zosimas and Sabbatius of Solovki and other buildings. The compositional centre of the monastery is a majestic five-tiered bell-tower dominating the entire area of the complex.

**The Trinity-St Sergius Monastery
The gate Church of St John the Forerunner. Interior**

**The Trinity-St Sergius Monastery
Cathedral of the Dormition. 1559–85
Chapel over the well. Late 17th century**

Альбом

МОСКВА

(на английском языке)

Издательство «Яркий город»
197101, Санкт-Петербург, Каменноостровский пр., д.15
тел./факс: (812)336-25-27, 336-25-28
www.yagorod.ru

Отпечатано в ООО «Первый издательско-
полиграфический холдинг», Санкт-Петербург

61 Cooperative Learning Activities in ESL

Charles Hirsch &
Deborah Beres Supple

J. WESTON
WALCH
PUBLISHER

PORTLAND, MAINE

Contents

II. HISTORY AND SOCIAL STUDIES 43

III. THINKING AND COMMUNICATING IN MATH .. 77

V. HEALTH, WELLNESS, AND SAFETY AND PREVENTION 121

Acknowledgments

To Lynn Perino, Assistant Superintendent of Curriculum and Instruction, and the Contra Costa County Office of Education for contributing their instructional and human resources and teaching ideas. Here's 61 thanks.

To the Teacher

61 Cooperative Learning Activities

These instructional strategies and interactive reproducibles help develop language acquisition using the most underused resource in the classroom: students, both second-language learners and native speakers, working together at mixed levels in the core curricula. All of these activities—some of them adapted from teaching strategies already used in the classroom and many others created out of our experiences with second-language learners—take a conversation-based cooperative learning approach for promoting language acquisition. Furthermore, this resource responds to an important trend in education that seeks integrating instruction so that students have opportunities to think, read, write, speak, and listen in each of the subject areas that they must master.

The rich content choices and the collaborative design of each activity encourage second-language students to participate with other limited-English students as well as with their English-speaking classmates. We've placed several activities in each section that can be used exclusively for language learning. If they seem to be remedial for some students, encourage your language-proficient students to be the teachers. (We all know how much we've learned by teaching!)

This resource is designed to be flexible. Some teachers may want to use these activities exclusively in ESL classes. Some teachers may want to use the activities in departmentalized classes with all their students. In nontraditional, restructured schools, teachers can use these teaching strategies in an interdisciplinary setting.

61 Activities to Support the ESL Learner

This book comes from our heartfelt belief, based on experience, that when we treat our newcomers to English as resources in the classroom, and not as problems, they not only succeed in learning English but also become part of our school community.

All students have a real need to belong. The newcomer students are no different, but we sometimes make them feel like outsiders. They may not show up in quite the latest styles, and they don't always use the current slang to let us know it, but they, too, want to be a part of something.

They come to our classrooms with expertise and skills in many areas, although they may not yet have enough English for us to test them. They also come to our schools from home cultures rich in history, stories, celebration, language, and literature. They *are* a part of something.

In *61 Cooperative Learning Activities in ESL*, we provide discussion, guided conversation, reading, and writing for ESL learners to use in the classroom and at school, and the activities will also make them feel at home in the community. We think this is a fair exchange for what they can contribute in the process of acquiring language. We set high, yet realistic expectations. And we give kids the care and support to succeed.

This care and support is fostered by working cooperatively in groups. In the case of ESL students, small group learning becomes a management technique to free up teachers to work individually with their limited-English students, to address their special needs. The teacher becomes the facilitator or, as we now say, "the guide on the side."

Some may think of this as the "warm and fuzzy" approach to education. We find that there is no more effective way to learn together, to provide the motivation that gets students excited about learning. It is our method for meaningfully assessing our students' strengths. It is truly "authentic assessment."

61 Strategies for Success

These activities provide you with 61 ways to engage your students. The activities are grouped into five sections:

    I. Language and Literature

    II. History and Social Studies

    III. Thinking and Communicating in Math

    IV. Thinking and Communicating in Science and Technology

    V. Health, Wellness, and Safety and Prevention

Each activity is designed to incorporate one or more elements of effective holistic teaching and learning.

- **Content** Newcomers to English are introduced to core subject areas and prepared for grade-level work with their native-speaking classmates.

- **Problem solving** Students work on finding a solution or performing a task, incorporating a variety of strengths and interests. Your challenge as teachers is to get students so involved in the search for a solution or completing the task that the learning of English becomes a natural outgrowth, not a forced struggle.

- **Humanistic Learning** Sharing interests, feelings, and common human concerns is an integral part of this student-centered experience.

- **Games** Games make language acquisition while learning new concepts something that's engaging and sometimes even amusing. Games lower the anxiety level and often help second-language learners forget their struggle, so they feel freer to speak English easily and more automatically.

61 Strategies for Student-Centered Learning

The second-language learners in our classrooms take big risks adapting to a new school and learning an unfamiliar language. At first, they may only speak a common language of hopefulness and determination. With our help, these students will attempt to master the challenges of speaking and learning English, make new friends, and find the rewards they may gain as productive members of our democracy.

By providing opportunities to master language and content while working with partners and in groups, we provide a student-centered classroom. We help our ESL students express themselves, learn, and participate, and we develop the critical and creative thinking skills of our native and fluent speakers alike as each contributes her or his expertise and interests. We move beyond tolerance toward deep respect and appreciation of diversity, where it becomes truly part of the learning experience.

Lesson-Plan Format

Activities

Title: The title is given in two parts.

[ ] Connecting to Reading—*How to Tell a Book by Its Cover*

Part 1   Part 2

Part 1 is a prompt to the teacher, suggesting which content, subject area, language focus, or skill you can connect the activity to or integrate it with.

Part 2 is the name of the activity and its corresponding reproducible. (Some names may be more clever than others in our play with the language. Whenever possible, point out these nuances of American English.)

Acquiring Language Through . . . : This is a quick reference to the tactics and instructional devices we as second-language teachers routinely use to help promote English language acquisition or to shelter the instruction.

Objective(s): The objectives are stated in terms of language development and/or the content focus. Objectives for the activities are listed in the Contents to help you as you make your teaching choices.

Time Required: The pacing may vary from class to class depending on how students work and what kinds of related ideas you bring to the class. Cut the time short or extend the activity if students may profit from further practice or show continued interest.

Group Size: Determine group configurations according to the needs of your student population. Although you may want to assign traditional roles to the learning groups (such as reader, recorder, artist), be careful. Make sure the limited-English student does not consistently end up as the artist. Provide the necessary support to the individuals learning English so they can participate as active learners in their groups.

Materials Needed: Read through this section carefully to make sure you've prepared enough reproducibles for either individuals or the group. In listing other materials, we've taken every effort to help you create a stimulating classroom environment while knowing full well that there are budget limitations.

In your teaching supplies, have plenty of chart paper or butcher paper. They're essential for brainstorming, to create graphic organizers and make word banks, and to facilitate group work. Post them around the classroom to enliven a print-rich environment for language learning. (Because chart or butcher paper is a classroom essential, we don't list it in "Materials Needed." It's always needed on hand.)

Also have plenty of magazines, newspapers, brochures, photos, and realia. We recycle all kinds of print and visual materials to make language and learning comprehensible and exciting.

From the Bookshelf: If an activity requires a literature selection, we've included suggestions that are easily available and in print. (This section does not appear for every activity.)

Teacher-to-Teacher: We never seem to be able to say enough. Here are some of our own and our colleagues' terrific suggestions, variations, and extensions for making these activities even better. (This section does not appear in every activity.)

Teaching Process

The teaching process is divided into four steps. Add your own ideas and make changes as you find necessary.

• PREPARE

This section summarizes what you need to get ready before you begin working with the whole class. Although these are not elaborate preparations, you may find this is a "teachable moment" to work individually and converse with your pre- and early-production students while they help you gather class materials, write up flash cards, and generally become at home with you and their new classroom. Whenever possible, prepare transparencies of the reproducibles and other visuals. Use clear acetate sheets in a standard copy machine to make an inexpensive but high-quality classroom resource.

• INTRODUCE/MODEL

When you introduce an activity, model the task as much as possible. Show as you tell how to do the activity. Paraphrase and rephrase the lesson. Use an overhead projector to display transparencies of the reproducibles and give examples as you work through them step by step. Whenever possible, draw from your own experience, and always strive to keep the language as simple as possible to make the task comprehensible.

• TEACH/PRACTICE

At the heart of cooperative learning is a student-centered curriculum in which limited-English students mix with language-proficient students. This offers you the structure and the time to teach and/or practice individually while the more language-proficient students contribute by helping one another and their limited-English classmates as they think, speak, read, and write together.

• CONCLUDE/ASSESS

Suggestions to conclude each activity are provided throughout. However, a formal assessment component is not always provided. There is no better way to bring closure to student work and to provide an opportunity for self-assessment than by displaying or publishing the work in some form. You not only recognize individual successes but also foster a creative classroom environment where the newcomer students feel comfortable and eager to learn.

Reading Strategies

For reading activities or activities involving additional reading, we suggest that you follow the preferred reading strategies that work effectively for you. Following are four strategies that work well for us.

- ### THE THREE R'S—READ A LOT! READ ALOUD! READ AROUND!

The best strategy for developing reading comprehension is to require a substantial amount of high-quality reading appropriate to your individuel students. Until second-language learners can achieve sustained silent reading, read aloud to them. In groups, have the students read around the group, with each member taking a turn reading. When necessary, assist others in the group who need help.

- ### CHORAL AND REPEATED READING

Organize the reading, choosing parts to read as refrain, dialogue, and individual lines. Assign the parts to the group and to individuals, designing it to proceed cumulatively or in unison.

- ### PARTNER READING

Sometimes referred to as paired or buddy reading, this reading strategy works well when you establish a rapport between a fluent reader and one with limited English. The partners read aloud together. Corrections are made as necessary and then the partners continue reading together until the limited-English student can read alone. The teacher is then free to monitor both the interpersonal relations and the mastery of the reading and the concepts.

- ### JIGSAW

In this cooperative reading strategy, students become experts in a portion of the text and share that expertise first with their own group and then with other groups. This strategy helps cover significant amounts of and/or more challenging material in manageable periods of time. Assign each group a section of material to read. Prepare questions for each group to read and discuss. Have each group read their material either as a group or in partners. Assign a group expert to report to the class the main points of his or her group assignment. After this, each group reconvenes to summarize the entire reading and apply it to the activity.

I. LANGUAGE AND LITERATURE

1. Connecting to Language—
Finding Out About Words

Acquiring Language Through . . . : Rhyming words and generating vocabulary.

Objective: To facilitate speaking and writing simple sentences.

Time Required: One class period.

Group Size: Four to five students.

Materials Needed: Reproducible 1 (one per group).

Teacher-to-Teacher: Handle this activity with humor. It can be a great icebreaker for getting new students to work together and feel comfortable putting words into language.

Teaching Process

• **PREPARE** On the chalkboard or butcher paper, write the words *cool, in, line, skates*, or other one-syllable words that students frequently hear around your school.

• **INTRODUCE/MODEL** Go word by word through the one-syllable words you have written. Ask students to say the words together. Have students brainstorm all the words that rhyme with each listed word. List those rhyming words. If you hit an impasse, point to examples of or act out rhyming words.

Now, demonstrate how you can use any combination or number of words to make

sentences, of sense or nonsense. Many is the class that's said "Do more fun gore!"

Point out similar parts of speech in each of the sentences you make. Each one should have at least a subject and a verb.

• **TEACH/PRACTICE** Have students work in groups, using Reproducible 1. Make sure students understand the directions and the model.

• **CONCLUDE/ASSESS** As a class, create a combined word bank. Share the sentences with the whole class. Invite fluent speakers to respond to or to categorize the sentences. Then vote on the best, worst, and funniest.

Finding Out About Words

List words that rhyme with each number printed below, as the examples do.

one	two	three	four	five
fun	do	tree	more	dive
run	to	glee	gore	jive

Write on! Use the following spaces to make your words into sentences of any length. Can you think of more sentences that will fit in the spaces below? Write them on the back of this sheet, on plain paper, all over the chalkboard, or on recycled paper from the wastebasket.

_____

_____

_____

_____

_____

_____

_____

_____

_____

_____

2. Connecting to Language— Finding Out About School

Acquiring Language Through . . . : Naming, constructing maps, and using diagrams.

Objective: To familiarize new students with the names and places at school.

Time Required: One class period.

Group Size: Partners or small groups.

Materials Needed: Reproducible 2 (one per student); graph paper.

Teaching Process

• **PREPARE** Collect print materials about your school, such as yearbooks, photographs, floor plans, or evacuation plans.

• **INTRODUCE/MODEL** Take the students on a tour of the school or show them visuals that name important places at your school.

Review the names with the students by asking them such questions as, "Where is the gym? the bathroom?" and "Who teaches (works) in Room _____?" As you develop pattern responses, chart or write each place name on the chalkboard.

• **TEACH/PRACTICE** Familiarize students with Reproducible 2. Then have them work in partners or groups to list places at your school. Refer to

visual and printed realia when necessary to fill in the boxes.

If your school is large, you might assign different groups different areas such as the north wing, the south wing, or the first or second floor.

Have the students cut out the place names and arrange them on graph paper in a diagram in order to make a map of the school.

• **CONCLUDE/ASSESS** Use the diagrams or maps of the school to assess students' understanding of their surroundings. Ask questions, or have students repeat pattern sentences using the place names. While some students can carry on simple conversations, others may simply point to or draw responses on the diagram.

Reproducible 2

Finding Out About School

✎ Write the name of your school in the middle box. Write names of other places in your school in the places provided. Cut out the boxes and use them to make a map of your school.

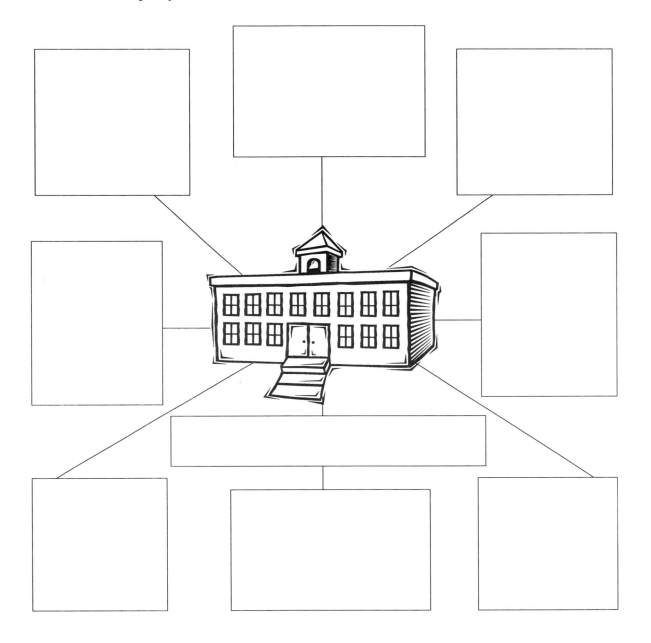

3. Connecting to Language—
Finding Out About the Class Schedule

Acquiring Language Through . . . : Diagrams, practicing telling time, and generating vocabulary through time and place.

Objective: To familiarize students with their school schedules.

Time Required: One class period.

Group Size: Four to six students.

Materials Needed: Reproducible 3 (one per student); large clock with movable hands; class schedule (one per student).

Teacher-to-Teacher: The first days at school for second-language learners can be puzzling. Perhaps you can work with other teachers to team up students from upper grades as school guides, offering advice, hospitality, and language assistance to your new students.

Teaching Process

• **PREPARE** Provide a large clock with movable hands. Copy a class schedule for each student.

• **INTRODUCE/MODEL** Begin by asking students to tell what time it is according to the classroom clock. Make a joke about being "clock-watchers," and explain what that means in English.

Move the hands on your demonstration clock and ask such questions as "What time is it?" "When does ESL class begin?" and "When is lunch?" Create pattern sentences using questions about time. Refer to copies of your class schedule to model and ask questions.

• **TEACH/PRACTICE** Pass out copies of Reproducible 3 to each student. Before group work, go through one or two examples with the whole class. Then have the students, in groups, draw in the times and complete their class schedules, helping each other. (You might substitute the actual schedules that some schools provide for students.)

• **CONCLUDE/ASSESS** Team up one of your ESL students with a language-proficient buddy. Go from group to group facilitating questions that will help your newcomers become comfortable with understanding their school day according to *where*, *when*, and *what* they are to do.

Group Names _____

Date _____

Reproducible 3

Finding Out About the Class Schedule

✎ What goes on during each period in your school day? On each clock, fill in the time when one of your class periods starts. In the box below each clock, write or draw what happens at that time.

1

2

3

4

5

✎ Complete your class schedule on this chart.

Period	Time	Event

4. Connecting to Language—
Finding Out About You

Acquiring Language Through . . . : Discussion and writing.

Objectives: To identify and name characteristics; to become acquainted with other students.

Time Required: One class period.

Group Size: Partners.

Materials Needed: Reproducible 4 (one per student).

Teacher-to-Teacher: You can adapt this activity and reproducible so that students can ask and answer the same kinds of questions about characters in a book.

Teaching Process

• **PREPARE** Prepare a transparency of Reproducible 4 or write the reproducible's questions on the chalkboard.

• **INTRODUCE/MODEL** Tell students that today's class will be a time to get to know each other. Use yourself as a model for answering the questions on Reproducible 4, making up conversations as you go along. Patterning the sentences from information on the reproducible, you might say things such as "My name is _____. I like _____. What do you like?"

• **TEACH/PRACTICE** Split the students up into partners. Give each student a copy of Reproducible 4, and make sure they understand the directions. Help facilitate conversations that use the information on the interview sheet.

• **CONCLUDE/ASSESS** Invite each student in the pair to introduce his or her partner to the class. Have students use the interview sheet as a guide to tell what they've learned about their classmate.

Make this into a cumulative game. Start with one student telling one thing about him/herself, then go to the next, who repeats that thing and adds on a fact about her/himself. Go around the classroom until you exhaust the possibilities.

Finding Out About You

Ask your partner the following questions to get to know him or her better. Then, have your partner ask you the same questions.

Name _____ **Age** _____

Address _____

Family members _____

What kind of animal would you like to be? _____

What's your favorite color? _____

What do you like in a friend? _____

What do you dislike most in this world? _____

What's the best thing you can do after school? _____

What's the last movie you saw? _____

When do you go to bed on school nights? _____

    On weekends? _____

When do you get up on school days? _____

    On weekends? _____

What's your favorite food? _____

Who's your favorite singer? _____ Your favorite group?

_____

What kind of work would you like to do? _____

_____

If you could be anything in the world, what would that be? _____

_____

Other questions: _____

_____

5. Connecting to Language—
P-E-O-P-L-E Spells B-I-N-G-O

Acquiring Language Through . . . : Generating vocabulary, dialogue, survey/interviews, and game playing.

Objectives: To appreciate individual differences; to identify character traits and background.

Time Required: One class period.

Group Size: Four or five students.

Materials Needed: Reproducible 5 (as many as necessary for each game); bingo prizes (optional).

Teaching Process

• **PREPARE** Prepare a transparency of Reproducible 5. Collect small prizes to reward winners.

• **INTRODUCE/MODEL** This activity is a great icebreaker for limited-English students. Use an overhead projector to show students the transparency of a blank bingo sheet. You may need to spend some time introducing the bingo game to them, demonstrating how they fill in the card and win by completing rows across, down, and vertically.

Use yourself as a model for filling in the bingo card. Write your own name in the middle square. Move around the room, finding students who match some of the descriptions in the other squares. Put each student's name in the appropriate square. Have students point to their physical characteristics when they are identified on the bingo card. Have others respond orally. You might have those

students stand who correctly fit the information called for on the bingo cards. Repeat the process until you come up with a completed row of squares.

• **TEACH/PRACTICE** Give each group a copy of Reproducible 5. Have each group work together to fill in their card. Have them fill in the middle square with your name, the name of their group, or your classroom number. Individual names can be repeated on each card. If the group can't seem to identify many characteristics, then combine groups.

• **CONCLUDE/ASSESS** Repeat the game with the whole class, but have a student take the role that you modeled. Have students use pattern sentences based on the information on the game board to tell about themselves, such as "I have black hair" or "I was born in Mexico."

Group Names _____

Date _____

P-E-O-P-L-E Spells B-I-N-G-O

B	I	N	G	O
I have eaten with chopsticks.	My mother's name begins with M.	I have at least one sister.	I am wearing at least two earrings.	I have blue eyes.
I have black hair.	I speak more than one language.	I am wearing a skirt.	I wear glasses.	I have seen the ocean.
I have walked in the snow.	I am wearing black pants.		I have a birthday in October.	I play soccer (football).
I am at least 6 feet tall.	I have a dog.	I have a cat.	I like to cook.	I am scared of mice.
I walk to school.	I ate an apple today.	My favorite color is purple.	My favorite food is pizza.	I have at least two brothers.

© 1996 J. Weston Walch, Publisher

11

61 Cooperative Learning Activities in ESL

6. Connecting to Language—
Following Directions

Acquiring Language Through . . . :   Planning, sequencing, and drawing and writing.

Objective: To tell and write sequenced directions for making something.

Time Required: One class period.

Group Size: Three to five students.

Materials Needed: Reproducible 6 (one per group). Ingredients for English muffin pizzas—use any kinds of sandwich or pizza foods that are available, such as one English muffin per group, cheese slices or cheese spread, and canned pizza sauce or presliced tomatoes; toaster oven or microwave; napkins; milk or juice; cups.

Teaching Process

• **PREPARE**   Gather all ingredients, but do not let the class see them. Select posters showing safety and emergency procedures.

• **INTRODUCE/MODEL**   Set the stage by personally relating anecdotes about the benefits of good, orderly directions, even to the point of saving other people's lives. Provide examples of print materials that show step-by-step procedures for dealing with an emergency, such as fire, choking, and evacuation. Have students point to and name the steps in numerical order.

Introduce the activity by telling students that what they'll do is not quite as serious, but that it will help them to practice following directions. If you feel your students are not familiar with the process, demonstrate the steps in making an English muffin pizza.

• **TEACH/PRACTICE**   Ask each group to fill out Reproducible 6. Be sure students understand the directions.

• **CONCLUDE/ASSESS**   Display the ingredients on a table. Have each group pass their written directions to another group so that each group has another group's directions. Tell each group to make their food according to the other group's directions. They must follow the directions **exactly**.

Once the groups have completed the task, go around the room and have them hold up what they made as they read the directions. As you bring closure, you might use this "teachable moment" to point out that we all interpret things differently. Clarify the importance of understanding that giving and following directions comes from seeing, speaking, and listening.

Finally, pour some milk or juice and enjoy the product of your work. Bon appetit!

Group Names _____

Date _____

Following Directions

How to make a _____

✏ Draw in order the steps for making an English muffin pizza. Then, go back and write the directions for each step on the lines under your drawings

7. Connecting to Language—
Kids Helping Kids

Acquiring Language Through . . . : One-to-one peer interaction, active listening, and generating vocabulary through discussion.

Objective: To establish a classroom-management and peer-support technique for working together and problem solving.

Time Required: Two class periods—one for getting acquainted, one to develop peer support and conclude. (Note: Once established, this activity can become an ongoing classroom practice.)

Group Size: Partners.

Materials Needed: Reproducibles 4 and 7 (one per student).

Teacher-to-Teacher: When given the chance, kids do an excellent job listening to, supporting, comforting, and helping each other. Research shows that peer support, particularly with immigrant and refugee students, can be both a means for modeling and practicing English and a technique to build cultural awareness and help reduce racial and other forms of conflict on campus. If you are interested in starting a formal peer program at your school, contact: National Peer Helpers Association, P.O. Box 3783, Glendale CA 91221-0783, (818) 240-2926.

Teaching Process

• **PREPARE** Take care in selecting partners and consider mixed abilities and diversity. Whenever possible, pair a language-proficient student with a pre- or early-production student.

Each student should also be given the opportunity to be the helper. Perhaps the pre-or early-production students are strong at math, physical education, or art, where English is not as critical.

• **INTRODUCE/MODEL** Group partners. Introduce yourself and each person, one to another. Shake hands. Make formal introductions. Tell them that this is their buddy for the term. Explain that he or she will help the other with homework, some decision-making that goes on in your school and

class, language difficulties, and just getting around in middle school.

• **TEACH/PRACTICE** Give each student a copy of Reproducibles 4 and 7. Model a conversation, using the getting-to-know-you questions on Reproducible 4 as a guide. Once partners have gotten acquainted through their conversation, then turn to Reproducible 7. Make sure students understand the directions for using the reproducible to identify ways in which partners can help each other throughout the school year.

• **CONCLUDE/ASSESS** Invite partners to share with the class ways in which they plan to help each other through the school year.

Kids Helping Kids

✎   Ask your buddy to tell you about the following. Write about it on the lines provided.

What subject areas in school would you like some help with at times? _____

_____

_____

What kind of help would be best for you? _____

_____

_____

What would you like to know about your school life (student activities, sports, teachers)?

_____

_____

_____

_____

What would you like to know about your community? _____

_____

_____

_____

_____

What are your strengths? What kinds of help do you think you could give to your buddy?

_____

_____

_____

_____

8. Connecting to Reading—
A Poster Dictionary

Acquiring Language Through . . . : Discussion, using manipulatives, writing, and relating pictures to words.

Objectives: To understand new words through context clues; to become familiar with and use a dictionary.

Time Required: One class period. This can be an ongoing activity, with students adding to this dictionary anytime they read.

Group Size: Four to six students.

Materials Needed: Reproducible 8 (one per student); literature/reading selections (one for modeling and one for each group, preferably chosen from subject area materials); a picture collection from newspapers, magazines, brochures, and other realia; scissors; glue or tape; poster board.

Teacher-to-Teacher: At regular intervals throughout the term, choose students to take charge of creating new pages for the poster dictionary with whatever new readings you encounter.

Teaching Process

• **PREPARE** Write on the chalkboard: *Word, What the Word Might Mean*, and *Why?*

Collect picture realia from such sources as magazines, newspapers, and brochures. Select any short, engaging reading selection that contains unfamiliar vocabulary. Select at least one word from this selection for modeling this activity, and make sure you have a picture that illustrates that word. Display a large sheet of poster board.

• **INTRODUCE/MODEL** Before you begin your reading, explain that one way to learn a new word when reading it is to guess the meaning of the word through its context, by using the words surrounding it to figure it out. One way to remember that word is to illustrate it by making a poster-size dictionary.

On the chalkboard, write the new word from the reading that you are introducing. After you read the passage, ask what the new word means. Write down the students' guesses under "What the Word Might Mean." Then ask the students "Why?" Help them decipher the meaning based on what they hear. Write those responses under "Why?"

Invite early-production students to act out their understanding of the word. Validate all responses as long as there is some justification from context, thereby supporting what new language learners are continually learning from context. Have volunteers look up the word in the dictionary, read it, then write it on poster board. Have a pre- or early-production student cut out a picture of the definition and paste it on the poster board.

• **TEACH/PRACTICE** Distribute Reproducible 8 to each group. Have students repeat the process you've just modeled. You might have language-proficient students read the new passage, record responses, and help with dictionary work, while pre- and early-production students might illustrate the context clues and meanings and label the words on the poster dictionary.

• **CONCLUDE/ASSESS** Ask language-proficient students to define their word(s) by sharing their poster dictionaries with the whole class. Pre-production students can point to their picture while a language-proficient student defines it orally.

A Poster Dictionary

Word   **What the Word Might Mean**

```
┌──────────────────────┐     _____
│                      │
└──────────────────────┘     _____
```

Why? _____

_____

Word   **What the Word Might Mean**

```
┌──────────────────────┐     _____
│                      │
└──────────────────────┘     _____
```

Why? _____

_____

Word   **What the Word Might Mean**

```
┌──────────────────────┐     _____
│                      │
└──────────────────────┘     _____
```

Why? _____

_____

Word   **What the Word Might Mean**

```
┌──────────────────────┐     _____
│                      │
└──────────────────────┘     _____
```

Why? _____

_____

✎   Use this worksheet to plan your Poster Dictionary. As you read and come to a new word, write it down on the line under **Word**. Then, in your own words, describe what you think the word means under **What the word might mean**. Also, explain how you figured out the meaning under **Why?**

✎   Now, using a piece of poster board, write down the word and its meaning. Also, draw a picture or cut one out of a magazine to illustrate the word.

9. Connecting to Reading—How to Tell a Book by Its Cover

Acquiring Language Through . . . : Role-playing, cloze work, and reading aloud.

Objectives: To recognize nouns and adjectives; to identify character traits.

Time Required: One class period.

Group Size: Partners.

Materials Needed : Reproducible 9 (one for each partner group); a core literature book for middle school, such as *Sarah, Plain and Tall*; *All Creatures Great and Small*; *Little Women*; or *Men of Iron*.

Teaching Process

• **PREPARE** Choose and display a core literature book that's grade-level appropriate. Write the title of the book that you're featuring on the chalkboard.

• **INTRODUCE/MODEL** Read the title together. To assess understanding, have early- and pre-production students role-play the title.

Erase one word in the title. Brainstorm any words (not just synonyms) that can substitute for the missing word: *Sarah, _____ and Tall*. Encourage limited-English students to act out and call out responses, while the more language-proficient students can write their suggestions on the board. Repeat the process for other words in the title.

• **TEACH/PRACTICE** Distribute copies of Reproducible 9 to each student and review its directions. Have students work in partners.

• **CONCLUDE/ASSESS** Share titles and illustrations with the class. When possible, show the original covers of those books listed on the reproducible. Ask the students to point to, tell, or act out the book title based on their understanding of the words and pictures on the cover.

Partners' Names _____

Date _____

How to Tell a Book by Its Cover

✎   Read the titles. Choose words to replace the words in the boxes. Write down all you can think of in the spaces provided.

Sarah, | Plain | and | Tall |

_____ _____
_____ _____
_____ _____
_____ _____
_____ _____

| Little | Women

_____
_____
_____
_____
_____

All Creatures | Great | and | Small |

_____ _____
_____ _____
_____ _____
_____ _____
_____ _____

Men of | Iron |

_____
_____
_____
_____
_____

Now that you've written the titles for a whole new set of books, let's show what these books might look like. Draw a book cover for your favorite title, either here or on a separate sheet of paper.

61 Cooperative Learning Activities in ESL

10. Connecting to Reading— A Problem-Solution Journal

Acquiring Language Through . . . : Journal writing, linking problem solving to personal experiences, and conversation.

Objectives: To analyze problems and solutions in literature; to foster multicultural awareness.

Time Required: Two class periods—one to introduce and model, one to teach, practice, and conclude.

Group Size: Partners. (If possible, one fluent speaker paired with an ESL student.)

Materials Needed: Reproducible 10 (one per partner group).

From the Bookshelf: Choose books that may prompt your students to talk about their own problems or those faced by their friends, their experiences with cross-cultural understanding, or with their adapting to life in the United States. The following three books are recommended because they're readily available in bookstores and libraries:

I Hate English, by Ellen Levine, illustrated by Steve Bjorkman. Scholastic, 1989. (A Chinese girl has problems learning English.)

Angel Child, Dragon Child, by Michelle Maria Surat, illustrated by Vo-Dinh Mai. Raintree, 1983. (A Vietnamese girl and an American boy play out "good girl, bad boy" surprisingly resolved in friendship and understanding.)

Encounter, by Jane Yolen, illustrated by David Shannon. Harcourt Brace Jovanovich, 1992. (A Taino Indian boy tells of what befalls his island of San Salvador when the Spaniards arrive.)

Teaching Process

• **PREPARE** Draw the chart on Reproducible 10 on the chalkboard. Choose a reading selection that is relevant to your student population in which your students can easily see a problem and its solution.

• **INTRODUCE/MODEL** Read one of the selections. Use the book as a springboard. Set up the problem, such as how it feels to move to another country or how others might feel or react if they came to a new country as immigrants or as invaders. Prompt students to use their own or their family's experiences when they came to the United States.

Chart the problems on the problem side of the chalkboard chart. Then examine how the characters in the book or the students themselves solved the problems. Record solutions on the chart on the chalkboard.

• **TEACH/PRACTICE** Read a different literature selection aloud, or ask students to think about the problem of any group of newcomers to America, such as the difficulties in speaking English, getting services, and finding one's way around school. Distribute a copy of Reproducible 10 to each pair of partners. Make sure they understand the directions and the process.

• **CONCLUDE/ASSESS** Open this to a class discussion. Have pairs share their experiences or problems. Then, as a class, have individuals offer solutions. Compare these with what the partners did together.

A Problem-Solution Journal

✎ What problems does someone new to this country face?

✎ Write or sketch the problem on the left-hand side of the chart below.

✎ Solve the problem.

✎ Write or sketch the solution on the right-hand side of the chart below.

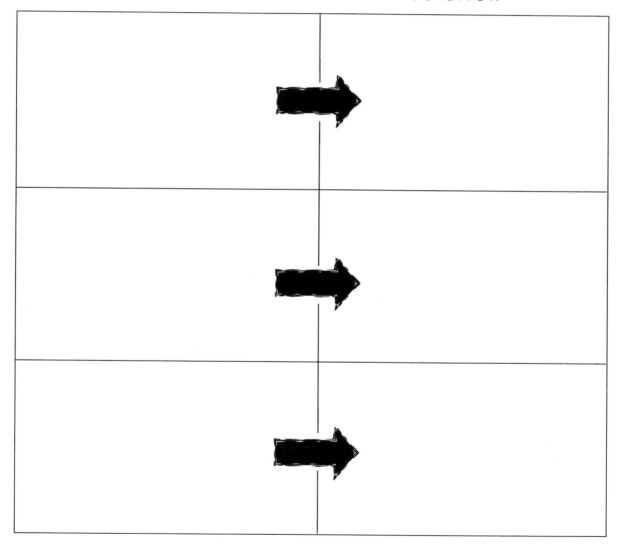

Problem   Solution

11. Connecting to Reading— Fairy Tales, Stuff, and Nonsense

Acquiring Language Through . . . : Recognizing and practicing dialogue through storytelling and role-playing.

Objectives: To practice introductions; to identify the main character in a story.

Time Required: Three class periods.

Group Size: Four to six students.

Materials Needed: Reproducible 11 (one for every two students); two classic fairy tales, available in anthologies or separately in picture books.

From the Bookshelf: Middle school students can have a good time comparing a familiar fairy tale with any of the following stories.

Cinder Edna, by Ellen Jackson, illustrated by Kevin O'Malley. Lothrop, Lee and Shepard, 1994.
The Cowboy and the Blackeyed Pea, by Tony Johnston. Putnam, 1992.
The Jolly Postman or Other People's Letters, by Janet and Allan Ahlberg. Little, Brown, 1986.
Ruby, an Urban Red Riding Hood Story, by Michael Emberly. Little, Brown, 1990.
Sidney Rella and the Glass Sneaker, by Bernice Myers. Macmillan, 1986.
The True Story of the Three Little Pigs, by A. Wolf, as told to John Scieszka. Viking Kestral, 1989.

Teaching Process

• **PREPARE** Draw a large Venn diagram on chart or butcher paper.

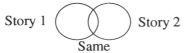

Label the left circle with the name of the first story and the right with the name of the second story.

• **INTRODUCE/MODEL** Read the first selection. Analyze the story by identifying the characters. List them next to the left circle. After more discussion, have an early- or pre-production student circle the main character. Then read the second selection and do the same.

At the next class period, compare and contrast the stories. Brainstorm what things the two stories have in common. List those elements where the Venn diagram intersects. Then look at the differences between story 1 and story 2. List those in their respective circles on the diagram.

Using the characters and situations in the stories, role-play and practice familiar language patterns. For example, introduce one character from one story to a character in another. Have students take on the roles of individual characters and interview one another; ask directions from one another; debate; ask *who, what, when, where, why,* and *how* questions.

• **TEACH/PRACTICE** Pass out Reproducible 11. Make sure the students understand the directions. Divide the class into groups. Have them first work in partners to make up a conversation between two characters, one from each story. You may need to provide real-life prompts (they introduce themselves; one finds the other stealing his/her wallet; they invite each other to a party; they ask directions). Then have the group combine conversations into a short skit.

• **CONCLUDE/ASSESS** Have students perform the skits. Discuss how points of view change from story to story and from group to group.

Group Names _____

Date _____

Fairy Tales, Stuff, and Nonsense

✎ One partner draws a character from story #1 on the lower left side of this page.

✎ The other student draws a character from story #2 on the lower right side.

✎ Write a conversation that the characters might have with each other.

✎ Share those conversations with your group. As a group, plan a skit of the conversation, practice it, and present it to the class.

Character 1   **Character 2**

12. Connecting to Reading Books—
Setting the Story Straight

Acquiring Language Through . . . : Manipulating and sequencing visuals, predicting outcomes, and summarizing, telling, or writing a story.

Objective: To determine the sequence of a story using picture-book illustrations.

Time Required: One to two class periods to introduce and teach. One class period to conclude and share stories.

Group Size: Five or six students.

Materials Needed: Reproducible 12 (one per group); two picture books; tape recorder (optional).

From the Bookshelf: The following picture books are recommended. You may also use your personal favorites for this activity.

Flight: the Journey of Charles Lindbergh, by Robert Burleigh, illustrated by Mike Wimmer. Philomel Books, 1991.

Life Doesn't Frighten Me, poem by Maya Angelou, painting by Jean-Michel Basquiat. Stewart, Tabori & Chang, 1993.

Saint George and the Dragon, retold by Margaret Hodges, illustrated by Trina Schart Hyman. Little, Brown, 1984.

Teaching Process

• **PREPARE** Reproduce the illustrated pages in two picture books you have selected by taking apart a book and laminating the illustrations. Cover up only the text before reproducing that page. Write two columns on the chalkboard, labeled *Number* and *Event.*

• **INTRODUCE/MODEL** Set the stage for this activity by telling students that they'll be making up their own story for an already published book. Shuffle the illustrations you've copied. Then display them.

Select volunteers to put the illustrations in an order that tells a story. When necessary, facilitate the process by pointing out such picture clues as changes of time, cause and effect, and dramatic progression. Encourage those with limited English to move the pictures around while others tell what is happening.

When you reach agreement, number the pictures. Write the number in the number column. Have volunteers tell or act out what event is happening. List those responses in the event column. Using those events, you may model telling the story that you've sequenced. Follow with volunteers retelling it. Then read the original story.

• **TEACH/PRACTICE** Distribute a set of shuffled illustrations from the second picture book along with Reproducible 12. Make sure students understand the directions, and have them proceed.

• **CONCLUDE/ASSESS** You may wish to tape-record the students' storytelling for assessment purposes as well as to encourage their speaking. Conclude by reading the original story to the class. Comparisons between the student work and the original story will underscore how many interpretations can be made from the same picture book.

Setting the Story Straight

✎ Place the pictures in order and number them. Write each number in the number column. Then, in the EVENT column, write down what is going on in each picture next to its NUMBER.

NUMBER	EVENT

✎ Now, use your number, pictures, and your EVENT information to write a story on the lines below.

STORY

_____

_____

_____

_____

_____

_____

_____

_____

_____

_____

13. Connecting to Reading Books— The Case of the Missing Character

Acquiring Language Through . . . : Generating vocabulary through reading and discussion, and creating character maps.

Objective: To analyze a character.

Time Required: Three class periods—one to introduce and model, one to teach and practice, one to conclude.

Group Size: Four to six students.

Materials Needed: Reproducible 13 (one per group); drawing supplies such as crayons, colored pencils, and marking pens; two books you have selected (see below).

From the Bookshelf: The following picture books are recommended for their character development. You may also use your personal favorites for this activity.

Chanticleer and the Fox, adapted from Geoffrey Chaucer's *Canterbury Tales* and illustrated by Barbara Cooney. Harper Trophy, 1989.

Mufaro's Beautiful Daughter, an African Tale, by John Steptoe. Lothrop, Lee & Shepard, 1987.

The Girl Who Loved Caterpillars: A Twelfth-Century Tale from Japan, adapted by Jean Merrill, illustrated by Floyd Cooper. Philomel Books, 1992.

Teaching Process

• **PREPARE** Select a picture book or chapter of a story to read to the class and a picture book or chapter of a story for each group to read. On the chalkboard or chart paper, write: *appearance, actions, other characteristics*.

• **INTRODUCE/MODEL** Read a picture book or chapter of a story in which the characters are strongly developed.

Tell the students to imagine that one of the characters has turned up missing, and it's their job to design a "Missing Persons" poster for that character. However, they must use words, not pictures, to describe the character.

Refer to the categories you've written on the chalkboard. Brainstorm how the students would characterize the missing person, using words to describe his/her: 1) appearance, 2) actions, and 3) other characteristics or word clues. Revisit the book as much as necessary. Whenever possible, help students categorize what they've described in

"other characteristics," such as mood, likes, and dislikes.

• **TEACH/PRACTICE** Pass out copies of Reproducible 13 and a selected reading to each group. As you model, have a student read through the book as many times as necessary. Have students brainstorm and complete the reproducible, challenging themselves to choose a character who's not obvious. Early-and pre-production students can point to clues of characterization and actions shown in the illustrations, while the language-proficient students are recorders.

• **CONCLUDE/ASSESS** Have each group exchange their reading selections and character descriptions. Before a new group reads the selections, have the group members guess the character based on the written descriptions and on thumbing through and looking at the illustrations. Then have them verify their answer by reading the text. Finally, have the group draw the character in the space provided. You might even offer a reward to the person who finds the character.

Group Names _____

Date _____

Reproducible 13

The Case of the Missing Character

✎   Fill in words to describe your character's **appearance**, **actions**, and **other characteristics**. Exchange with another group and have them guess the missing characters.

APPEARANCE

_____
_____
_____
_____
_____
_____
_____
_____
_____

ACTIONS

_____
_____
_____
_____
_____
_____
_____
_____
_____

OTHER CHARACTERISTICS

_____
_____
_____
_____
_____

MISSING

??????????????????
?   ?
?   ?
?   ?
????????? ??????

14. Connecting to Reading Books—
The Cover-Up

Acquiring Language Through . . . : Writing English, discussion, and role-playing.

Objectives: To write and tell a story; to understand parts of a book.

Time Required: Two class periods.

Group Size: Four to six students.

Materials Needed: Reproducible 14 (one per group); a big book; book jackets (one per group); sentence strips or gummed labels; tape recorder (optional); writing paper; marking pens, art supplies.

Teaching Process

• **PREPARE** Select a book with an interesting cover. Use a sentence strip, gummed label, or paper to cover up the title only. Follow the same procedure for each book jacket, (one per learning group).

• **INTRODUCE/MODEL** Display the cover of the big book. Brainstorm what the students see in the picture. Ask students such questions as "What is happening?" and "Who are the characters?" Generate responses from early-production students by having them point to a character. For example, you might name an obvious feature of a character shown on the cover (e.g., smiling). Then have the student point to the character who's smiling. Have a recorder write down responses on the chalkboard or chart paper.

Tell the students you will begin a story and that they'll go "round robin" to continue the story. Advise students to use any of the information supplied during the brainstorming to shape their part of the story. They may also ask any questions of the previous storyteller to clarify meaning. Model the procedure by beginning the story.

Keep a record of each segment of the story as you go along. Have a student record it in longhand, tape-record it, or have a transcriber input it on the computer. After you help bring the story to a close, put the story together in written form and read it back to the class.

• **TEACH/PRACTICE** Pass out copies of the book covers to each group. Have the students analyze the cover in the ways that you modeled, using the reproducible to organize their thinking. Check that they understand the instructions. After sufficient discussion and writing, ask the students in each group to number off. (It's best to start with a fluent speaker.) Have the first student write and tell his or her part of the story, then pass it to the next person. Continue the exchange several times.

• **CONCLUDE/ASSESS** Follow up by having each group edit their story and prepare it for publication and oral presentation. Encourage them to give their story a title. (Refer them to the bottom section on the reproducible.)

Group Names _____

Date _____

The Cover-up

✎ Who are the characters on the book cover? What are they doing? What's happening? Record your group ideas here.

Who?
_____
_____
_____
_____

What are they doing?
_____
_____
_____

What's happening?
_____
_____
_____
_____

What's the title of your story? Write it in the space below. Cut it out and attach it to the book cover.

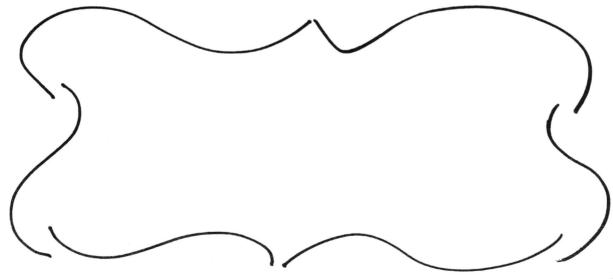

15. Connecting to Reading Poetry—
Can You Repeat That?

Acquiring Language Through . . . : Generating vocabulary through writing a story poem, choral speaking/chanting, and total physical response.

Objectives: To identify parts of speech; to a reword a poem.

Time Required: One to two class periods.

Group Size: Partners.

Materials Needed: Reproducible 15 (one per partner group).

Teacher-to-Teacher: You might suggest that students replace the circled words on the reproducible by category—for example, substitute *house* with names of buildings or places at school; *cheese* with names of other foods; *cat* with names of other pets.

Teaching Process

• **PREPARE** Prepare a transparency of Reproducible 15, or write the poem on the chalkboard or chart paper.

• **INTRODUCE/MODEL** Invite students to read, chant, or rap the poem "This Is the House That Jack Built." You might create a beat as you read it so students can move and dance to the chant-like reading.

• **TEACH/PRACTICE** Going word by word, replace such words in the title as *This* with other pronouns, *House* with other names of things, and *Jack* with other proper nouns. Have more fluent speakers identify the parts of speech. Have early-

production students find examples of the words in magazines and books. Repeat, read, chant, or rap each time you put a new word in place. Have fun with this process.

Distribute and review Reproducible 15. Make sure students understand the directions before proceeding.

• **CONCLUDE/ASSESS** Depending on the level of your students, use the reworded poems (both written and spoken) to assess how students understand and restate language, use words in context, and identify parts of speech.

Can you repeat that?

✎ Read the poem aloud with your partner.

The (House) That (Jack) (built)

This is the (house) that (Jack) (built.)

This is the (cheese)
That lay in the (house) that (Jack) (built.)

This is the (mouse) that ate the (cheese)
That lay in the (house) that (Jack) (built.)

This is the (cat) that killed the (mouse)
That ate the (cheese)
That lay in the (house) that (Jack) (built.)

This is the (dog) that scared the (cat)
That killed the (mouse)
That ate the (cheese)
That lay in the (house) that (Jack) (built.)

✎ Now, create your own poem by replacing the words that are circled with your own words. Write on the back of this paper or on another sheet of paper.

16. Connecting to Reading Poetry— Pictures Say a Thousand Words

Acquiring Language Through . . . : Visualizing, word-picture relationships illustrating text, and noting details.

Objective: To create pictures to match the text of a poem.

Time Required: One to two class periods.

Group Size: Four to six students.

Materials: Reproducible 16 (one per student and one per group); Reproducible 15 (the original or a student version) or a poem you choose (one for modeling and another one for each group); poster board, chart or butcher paper, and art/drawing supplies as necessary to make big books.

From the Bookshelf: If you do not use a student-generated poem such as one created in Activity 15, choose a poem that is visually strong or rich in narrative. These are a few suggestions found in many middle school anthologies: "America the Beautiful," by Katherine Lee Bates; "Knoxville, Tennessee," by Nikki Giovanni; "Stopping by Woods on a Snowy Evening," by Robert Frost.

Teacher-to-Teacher: As an end product, have students share their big books with students in the lower grades. We have noticed that early-production students feel less inhibited reading aloud to younger students. This way, too, we find that what may appear as remedial to some students becomes a meaningful, purposeful activity.

Teaching Process

• **PREPARE** Set out art supplies and make copies of two poems—one copy for introducing and modeling and a copy of another poem(s) for each group.

• **INTRODUCE/MODEL** If you have done Activity 15, you might use a student's version of "This Is the House That Jack Built." Otherwise, tell students they'll illustrate a poem, creating a picture to match the text. Read through the model poem once. Then have the students read through the model poem with you as necessary for comprehension. Discuss, and act out the poem verse by verse.

Distribute a copy of Reproducible 16 to each student. To help check for meaning and to facilitate visual thinking, have students use the frames of the story board on Reproducible 16 to sketch the development of the model poem. Proceed verse by verse or at other points of entry.

• **TEACH/PRACTICE** Distribute another copy of Reproducible 16 to each group along with the copy of the poem you want students to illustrate. Make sure they understand the directions, and have them work in groups.

• **CONCLUDE/ASSESS** In most groups, one student is more artistically adventurous than others, so configure your groups accordingly. Have students use Reproducible 16 for design and text ideas to enlarge into "big books."

Have the students share their illustrated texts with the class. Use the big books together with Reproducible 16 to assess students' progress as you evaluate their ability to sequence and associate word meaning with visuals.

Group Names _____

Date _____

16. Pictures Say a Thousand Words

✎ How many pictures do you need to illustrate a poem?

✎ Decide on each part of the poem you want to draw. Write those lines under each box below or on separate paper.

✎ Sketch the picture that goes with those lines of poetry.

_____ _____ _____

_____ _____ _____

_____ _____ _____

_____ _____ _____

_____ _____ _____

_____ _____ _____

✎ Use your ideas on this sheet to create a "big book" of your illustrated poem.

17. Connecting to Reading Newspapers— From the Front Page

Acquiring Language Through . . . : Using newspapers to provide a purpose for reading, and discussion.

Objectives: To activate and validate prior knowledge; to provide ways to summarize new learning.

Time Required: One class period.

Group Size: Four to six students.

Materials Needed: Reproducible 17 (one per group); marking pens; two front-page newspaper articles—one of them copied for each group.

Teaching Process

- **PREPARE** To keep a record of your work, prepare a *K-W-L* chart and post it in the classroom. Use Reproducible 17 as a sample. Select newspaper articles that are timely and filled with facts.

- **INTRODUCE/MODEL** Explain that you'll read a factual newspaper article to the class. If necessary, clarify what you mean by "fact" versus "fiction" or "opinion."

  Identify the topic of the article. You might also point out such journalistic features as the headline and byline. Brainstorm what the students already know about the article, and write their responses under "*K*" on your chart.

  Encourage students to think about and then brainstorm what they would like to find out, and write those responses under "*W*" on your chart.

  Read the article aloud. Have students brainstorm what they learned from reading the article, and write those responses under "*L*" on your chart.

- **TEACH/PRACTICE** Introduce the topic for another newspaper article.

  Distribute one copy of Reproducible 17 to each group. Be sure students understand the directions. Have groups brainstorm what they know ("*K*") and what they want to find out ("*W*").

  Read another newspaper article aloud to the class. Help early-production learners look for key words in the article. Have them circle those words. Have language-proficient students record group responses of what they've learned ("*L*").

- **CONCLUDE/ASSESS** Assign reporters from each group to share the conclusions about what they've learned. Most importantly, validate how much students already know about a topic, since speaking and reading a second language is often fostered by the prior knowledge that students bring to that experience.

Reproducible 17

From the Front Page

Fill in the chart as you think about what you know and what you want to find out about the topic chosen by your teacher. Then, read the article. Afterwards, fill in what you learned that you didn't know before.

K	W	L
What We Know	What We Want to Find Out	What We Learned

18. Connecting to Reading Newspapers— Comic Strip Conversations

Acquiring Language Through . . . : Conversation, role-playing, and using context clues.

Objectives: To create and practice conversation; to recognize written forms of dialogue.

Time Required: One class period.

Group Size: Four to six students.

Materials Needed: Reproducible 18 (three to four per group); two comic strips (three to four frames taken from newspapers or comic books); fine-point pens.

Teaching Process

• **PREPARE**   After making a copy of both original comic strips for reference, white-out or cover up the dialogue in each speech bubble. Use an enlarged version of one comic strip for modeling, and prepare copies of the other for each group. Also, prepare enlarged versions or overhead transparencies of Reproducible 18.

• **INTRODUCE/MODEL**   Display a blank comic strip with the dialogue covered up. Explain how the sequence of the cartoon story develops from frame to frame.

Ask such questions as "Who are the characters?" "What are they doing?" Elicit responses from early-production students by having them point to the characters and act out with other students what might be happening.

Model how to look for clues in the cartoon strip. Point out what you might predict from the characters' facial expressions, clothing, body language, and surroundings. Use the "Notes" section on Reproducible 18 to summarize your predictions and responses.

With your students, use these notes to create simple phrases or sentences for each bubble. Record these in the "Quotes" section on Reproducible 18. Transfer these quotes to the appropriate bubble in the comic strip.

Compare the class cartoon with the original. You may wish to look for similarities and differences.

• **TEACH/PRACTICE**   Pass out copies of the unused comic strip. Give each group one copy of Reproducible 18 for each frame of the comic strip. Have the students analyze the cartoon and write dialogue in the ways that you modeled. Encourage the early-production students to act out physically while the fluent speakers provide written and oral support.

• **CONCLUDE/ASSESS**   Have each group act out their responses. Assess their work by discussing how they used the illustrations in context to create the dialogue.

Comic Strip Conversations

 For each frame of the comic strip:

- Look at the frame.

- What do you think is happening in the frame? List what you think and see in the "Notes" column below.

- Write what the character might say in the "Quotes" column, based on what you think you see.

- Choose quotes from your list and write them in the appropriate speech bubbles in the comic strip.

FRAME NUMBER [ ]

NOTES	QUOTES
(What you think and see)	(What the characters say)

19. Connecting to the Media—
Advertising Addiction

Acquiring Language Through . . . : Analyzing advertising messages through the media, role-playing, and generating descriptive vocabulary.

Objectives: To infer some hazards of tobacco and alcohol use; to categorize an advertisement using *what* and *who*.

Time Required: Two class periods—one to introduce and one to teach and practice.

Group Size: Four to six students.

Materials Needed: Reproducible 19 (one per group); magazine ads for tobacco and alcohol.

Teaching Process

• **PREPARE** Select several tobacco and alcohol ads from magazines to display.

• **INTRODUCE/MODEL** Begin by discussing *how* tobacco and alcohol can affect a person's life. Focus the discussion on the effects on growing adolescents. Those concerns might be personal, such as how tobacco yellows the teeth or makes the breath smell bad, or the effects might be social, such as how alcohol can disrupt family life.

Choose an ad and examine it. Write the words *people, places,* and *things* on the chalkboard. Referring to these words, brainstorm what the students see in the ad. Point to such features as how the models in the ads look so healthy, young, and glamorous and how the locales are so beautiful. Ask students such questions as "Who are the people in the ads?" "What are they doing?" Write down the words the students associate with the ads.

Write the words *who* and *what* on the chalkboard. Conclude by asking, "To whom are they

advertising?" "What is the ad trying to do or accomplish?" List responses.

• **TEACH/PRACTICE** Pass out copies of the ads and Reproducible 19, one of each to each group. Go over the directions with the students. Have the students work in groups to analyze the ads. Refer to Reproducibles 9 and 15 if the students need more practice using descriptive words in context.

• **CONCLUDE/ASSESS** After the students have analyzed the ad, regroup. Have them think about how they might design an ad that shows what tobacco or alcohol really does. You may need to prompt them by offering some examples, such as picturing a model visiting a friend in the cemetery, or illustrating a family lost in argument, with overturned bottles and glasses in the scene.

Have each group display their ads around the school.

Advertising Addiction

✎   Look at the ad and think about this:

  • Who are the people in the ad?

  • What do the places in the ad look like?

  • What things do you see in the ad?

   List the answers to these questions below. List words that describe the people, places, and things in the ads.

People	Places	Things
_____	_____	_____
_____	_____	_____
_____	_____	_____
_____	_____	_____
_____	_____	_____

✎   Draw an ad that tells what really happens when you smoke, drink, and act stupid.

  • Who is the target of this ad? (To whom is the tobacco or alcohol company advertising?) Record your answer under "Who" below.

  • What is the ad trying to do or accomplish? Record your answer under "What" below.

   Now answer the questions.

Who	What
_____	_____
_____	_____
_____	_____
_____	_____

20. Connecting to the Media—
Sounds Good to Me

Acquiring Language Through . . . : Music and generating vocabulary through print advertising.

Objective: To understand and practice using opposites, comparison, and contrast.

Time Required: One to two class periods.

Group Size: Groups of five or fewer students.

Materials Needed: Reproducible 20 (one per group); a CD player or tape recorder (preferably one per group); a variety of music selections (two to model and one per group); newspaper and magazine ads for CDs and tapes.

Teaching Process

• **PREPARE** Choose two favorite CDs or tapes to introduce the activity. (Ask students for their favorites.) One should be up-tempo, maybe hard rock. The other should be quiet, easy listening. Also select a variety of recordings (classical, jazz, folk, rap). Ask volunteers to bring in CD players or tape recorders, one for each group.

• **INTRODUCE/MODEL** Play your first music selection. Pause. Then play your second selection. On the chalkboard or on butcher paper write **hard rock** and **soft sounds**.

Invite pre- and early-production students to show you how they felt while listening to the first and second selections. Write responses under the appropriate column. Then ask *when* or *where* they might listen to each selection and list those responses.

Invite students to point to, act out, or talk about the similarities and differences between the lists. Point out all the words (the situations, the feelings listed) that are opposites.

• **TEACH/PRACTICE** Display newspaper and magazine ads. Suggest that the students' job is to be a DJ. They have to create an intro or write an ad for one piece of music.

Distribute Reproducible 20. Make sure students understand the directions. Play a piece of music as the introduction to the activity.

• **CONCLUDE/ASSESS** Make individual lists of the words compiled on each group's reproducible. Facilitate comparisons and contrasts as part of the class discussion. Evaluate how the students are able to understand similarities and differences among each of the music selections. Invite each group to give a radio introduction to their music or display an ad for their song.

Sounds Good to Me

Listen to the song. Have each person in the group write or draw a word that describes the song in each space on the CD.

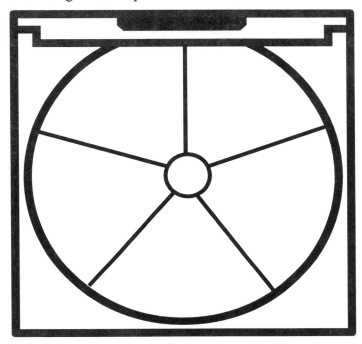

How would you announce this song on the radio? How would you advertise this song in the newspaper? Use the words from above to let us know.

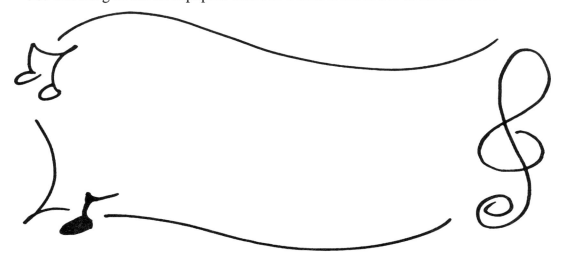

61 Cooperative Learning Activities in ESL

II. History and Social Studies

21. Historical Literacy— Lining Up History

Acquiring Language Through . . . : Discussion and graphic organizers.

Objectives: To understand the meaning of time and chronology; to use research and reference books.

Time Required: One class period to introduce and teach. One or more class periods for research, depending on students' ability and depth of study.

Group Size: Four to six students.

Materials Needed: Reproducible 21 (three to four per group); reference books, history texts, encyclopedias; blank roll of wide cash register tape or several strips of construction paper or sentence strips taped end-to-end.

Teacher-to-Teacher: Teachers find the time line to be one of the most helpful aids for visualizing and talking about historical time and sequence, particularly with limited-English students. As you study historical events throughout the school year, remember to plot them along the class time line. Refer to it often to assess immediately and summarize the historical events studied.

Teaching Process

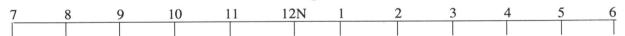

• **PREPARE** Assemble a giant time line for your classroom. Tape an unraveled blank roll of cash register tape around the room or create a long paper strip by taping construction paper or sentence strips end-to-end. Draw a time line on the chalkboard or on a separate large paper strip. Label it with several hours of the day, fixing noon as the central point.

• **INTRODUCE/MODEL** After explaining that history can be looked at like one long line of events, make a parallel with the students' day. Have volunteers write or draw an event that happens at each interval on the time line you've displayed. Have other students repeat the times of day and then name, act out, and/ or draw what they do at those times. Add the written responses to your time line.

As you make the transition to studying history, point out that students likewise can fill in the events of history along a line which we call a time line. On the roll of cash register tape, create a classroom time line. Point to 0 as the central point which marks the birth of Christ. Explain the division of history into anything before Christ's birth as B.C.

(or B.C.E.), and anything after Christ's birth as A.D. or C.E.

Brainstorm a few events that students know about, and plot those on the time line.

• **TEACH/PRACTICE** Pass out Reproducible 21, which students will use as a planning document. Make sure they understand the directions. Since the breadth of this activity is expansive, you may wish to assign it in various ways. Each group might take a range of years. You may wish to focus only on the time period students are studying at that grade level. You may proceed day to day throughout the school week covering a different span of time or historical period on each day.

• **CONCLUDE/ASSESS** Invite each group to plot the events they found on the class time line. Have them first point to where the events fell along the continuum of the time line. For accuracy, help students make corrections as necessary before they write and draw their events on the time line.

Group Names ______________________________

Date ______________________________________

Reproducible 21

Lining Up History

Fill in historical events and the date they happened.

Event from History	Approximate Date

Plot your events and the date they happened on the time line here.

Time Line

0 ____ Current Year

22. Historical Literacy— His Story/Her Story

Acquiring Language Through . . . : Role-playing and discussion.

Objectives: To ask, *who what, where, when, why,* and *how* questions; to examine historical point of view.

Time Required: Two class periods.

Group Size: Four to five students.

Materials Needed: Reproducible 22 (one per group); reading selections (see below).

From the Bookshelf: The following books are available through most bookstores. Each book provides a historical point of view through the eyes of a person in at least one of the commonly taught historical strands.

Ancient: *Greek Gods and Heroes,* by Alice Low, illustrated by Arvis Stewart. Macmillan, 1985.

World History: *Where Do You Think You're Going, Christopher Columbus?* by Jean Fritz. Putnam, 1980.

U.S. History: *Molly's Pilgrim,* by Barbara Cohen, illustrated by Michael J. Deraney. Lothrop, Lee and Shepard, 1983.

Modern: *The Day Martin Luther King, Jr., Was Shot: A Photo History of the Civil Rights Movement,* by Jim Haskins. Scholastic, 1992.

Teaching Process

• **PREPARE** Prepare an overhead transparency of Reproducible 22 or write the question words *who? what? when? where? why? how?* on the chalkboard.

Select an appropriate reading—either one that aligns with what students are studying in history or one that may be culturally relevant to your student population.

• **INTRODUCE/MODEL** Share a reading selection with the class. After the first reading, refer to the transparency or the chalkboard. Help students formulate questions that they might ask the character in the book. Create a series of questions, such as "Who were your parents?" "What made you leave

_____?" "When did you come to the United States?"

• **TEACH/PRACTICE** Assign students to work in groups to formulate their questions to ask the person from history they've read about. Give each group a copy of Reproducible 22. Make sure they understand the directions. Prompt them by suggesting that the person is in the room. Help them further by having one of the students act out that character.

• **CONCLUDE/ASSESS** Once the groups have formulated questions, ask a volunteer to become that character. Have the groups ask their questions, while the volunteer pretends he or she is that actual person from history.

Group Names _____

Date _____

His Story / Her Story

What do you want to know from his story/her story?

Ask _____ (his name/her name).

Make up at least 10 questions to ask the person from history that you read about. Write the questions on the lines below. Start each question with the word inside the box, as shown in the examples provided.

1. Who? (*Example:* Who were your parents?) Your question: _____

_____

_____

2. What? (*Example:* What made you leave your country?) Your question: _____

_____

_____

3. When? (*Example:* When did you come to the United States?) Your question:_____

_____

4. Where? (*Example:* Where did you go to school?) Your question: _____

_____

5. Why? (*Example:* Why did you become famous?) Your question: _____

_____

6. How? (*Example:* How did you earn a living?) Your question: _____

_____

_____

_____

Acquiring Language Through . . . : Generating vocabulary for words of time and place, using Venn diagrams, labeling and drawing, and total physical response.

Objective: To become familiar with and practice using cardinal directions.

Time Required: Two or three class periods.

Group Size: Four to six students.

Materials Needed: Reproducible 23A and 23B (one each per group); large sentence strips, 5" by 8" index cards, or strips cut from poster stock for labels.

Teacher-to-Teacher: Although the focus of this activity is simply using cardinal direction to analyze and discuss places around school and in your neighborhood, you may adapt it to use with many content areas in social studies. For example, compare weather in New York and Los Angeles, Minneapolis and Houston. Explore the differences of the U.S. Civil War. Use the East-West diagram to analyze the westward movement.

Teaching Process

• **PREPARE** Draw a giant Venn diagram similar to Reproducible 23A. Use two different colors of chalk to make the circles. Label one **North** and the other **South**.

• **INTRODUCE/MODEL**
Point to north and south on the Venn diagram, and then orient the students to north and south in your classroom. Have recorders write labels for these directions and invite pre- and early-production students to place them appropriately. Go around the room asking students to name things. After you correctly label them, transfer that information to your diagram. Place things in the middle of the room in the overlap area of the diagram. For example: Repeat the process for east and west, using both the same and different objects. Compare the diagrams.

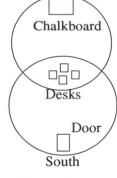

North

Chalkboard

Desks

Door

South

• **TEACH/PRACTICE** When possible, assign each group different areas of the school: a section outdoors or the lunchroom, gym, library, or media center. You may need to have assistants or more experienced students accompany each group. Establish north and south in each area and identify the middle area of overlap. Have each group complete Reproducible 23A in the way that you modeled, making sure they understand the instructions.

• **CONCLUDE/ASSESS** Have each group show and explain their Venn diagrams. Discuss differences and commonalities. Assess how well your students understand their relationship to directions by having them name, point to, and stand next to objects in that directional field.

Reassign the groups to different areas and have them map and then describe their school or neighborhood using Reproducible 23B for east and west.

Reproducible 23A

North * South

✎ Survey the area. Look around. Decide what goes in the middle overlap section of the diagram. Then decide if other things go in the north or south section of the diagram. Draw in what you see. Label the objects.

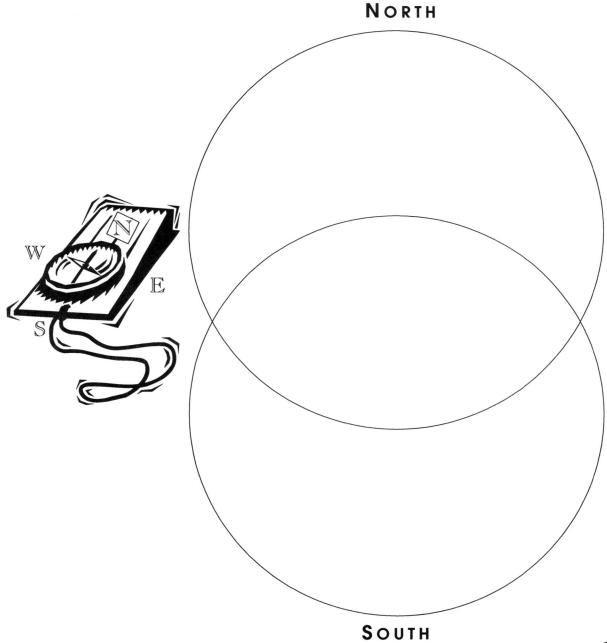

NORTH

SOUTH

Reproducible 23B

East * West

🖉 Survey the area. Look around. Decide what goes in the middle overlap section of the diagram. Then decide if other things go in the east or west section of the diagram. Draw in what you see. Label the objects.

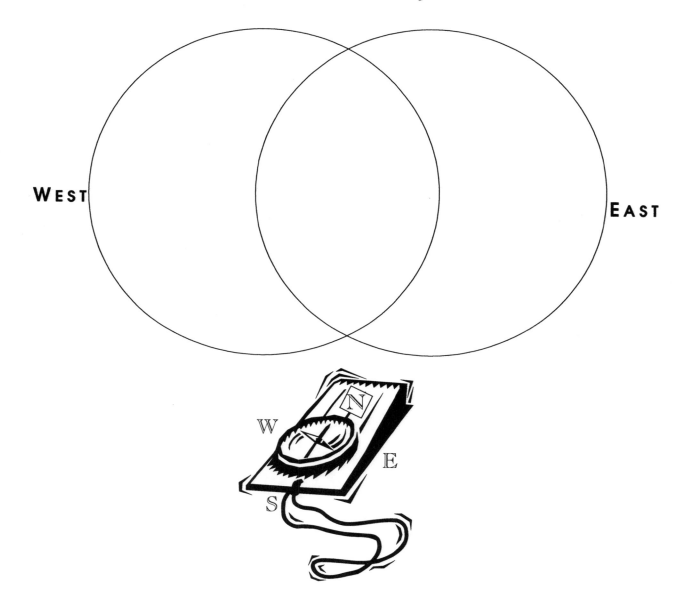

W E S T   E A S T

61 Cooperative Learning Activities in ESL

24. Geographical Literacy— City, Town, All Around

Acquiring Language Through . . . : Discussion, naming places, using maps to identify important places in the community, and total physical response.

Objective: To use *who, what,* and *where* questions in order to understand living together.

Time Required: Two class periods—one to introduce and teach, one to conclude.

Group Size: Six equal groups.

Materials Needed: Reproducible 24 (one per group); map of your city, town, or region; promotional materials, visitor information, and local newspapers with pictures of points of interest in your city, town, or region; colored marking pens; masking tape.

Teaching Process

• **PREPARE** On the chalkboard, draw a word web similar to the one on Reproducible 24. Prepare six sheets of chart or butcher paper. Label them: **food, clothing, shelter, health and safety, fun,** and **peace of mind**. Tape the sheets around the room.

   Display local maps. Gather pictures from promotional materials, visitor information, and local newspapers with pictures of points of interest in your city, town, or region.

• **INTRODUCE/MODEL** Begin by asking an early-production student to fill in the center of the word web with the name of your city or town. Then guide the students through examining each of the categories, starting with food. Pattern the brainstorming by asking *what, where,* and *who* questions, such as: "What is a place to go for food in our town?" "Where do you go for food in our town?" "Who sells you the food?"

   Before you break up into groups, list one or two items for each category on the word web. Draw in any necessary lines to make connections between the categories on the word web. Fill in the word

web and have volunteers write on the chart paper the places they brainstormed. Have others, particularly pre- and early-production students, point out those places on a map.

• **TEACH/PRACTICE** Distribute Reproducible 24. Go over any questions students may have about completing the work. When all groups have completed the reproducible, assemble the class and combine the lists. Add places to the charts displayed around the room.

• **CONCLUDE/ASSESS** Assign a category to each group. Give each group the corresponding chart paper for that category. Instruct each group to look through the brochures and realia to collect pictures as well as draw illustrations of the places named in the category for their group. (For example, one group may have the category *fun* in which they'll find or draw pictures of playgrounds, parks, and the mall.) Tape each piece together to make a collage of your city. Refer often to this collage to help pre- and early-production students become familiar with places in your community.

51

Group Names ______________________________

Date ______________________________

Reproducible 24

City, Town, All Around

✎ Where do you go? List their names under each category. Find those places on a map.

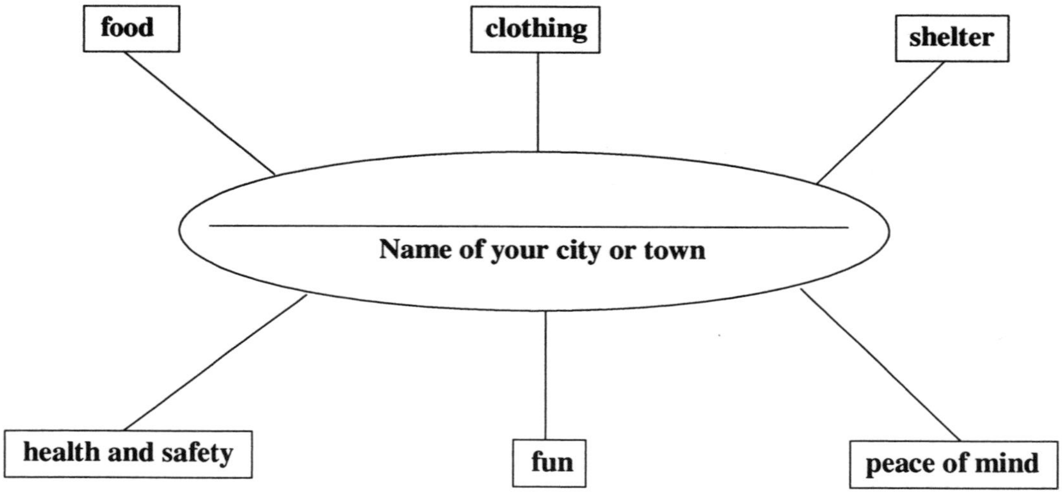

food
clothing
shelter
Name of your city or town
health and safety
fun
peace of mind

25. Social-Political Literacy— Wants and Needs

Acquiring Language Through . . . : Conversation and writing.

Objectives: To distinguish between *wants* and *needs*; to promote attitudes and behaviors that foster good citizenship.

Time Required: Two class periods.

Group Size: Five equal groups.

Materials Needed: Reproducible 25 (one per group).

Teaching Process

• **PREPARE** Write a copy of the Reproducible 25 chart on the chalkboard.

• **INTRODUCE/MODEL** Choose one of the following categories from Reproducible 25, or select a branch of government to brainstorm: **federal government, local government, education, family,** or **environment.** Brainstorm what the students *want* in that particular category in order to have a full, productive life. Then ask what they *need.*

Facilitate early- and intermediate-production students' understanding of wants (explaining that this is what they like or that may improve their life) and needs (explaining that this is what is necessary). Move students' suggestions from one column to the other as you reach agreement on what is a need and what is a want.

Now brainstorm ways in which the students can provide for the needs, or some of them, that

they have named. Elicit suggestions as to what people or agencies (governmental and non-governmental) could provide for the needs, and how they can do it. Record these suggestions under "Others" and "How to Provide."

Then elicit suggestions as to how students themselves could provide for the needs. Record these ideas under "Self " and "How to Provide."

• **TEACH/PRACTICE** Distribute Reproducible 25. Make sure students understand the directions. Assign each group one of the categories listed on the reproducible (but not one you have modeled). Work with groups to distinguish the wants and/or needs in their category.

• **CONCLUDE/ASSESS** Have each group share their conclusions and add new ones where necessary.

53

Group Names _____

Date _____

Wants and Needs

✎ Circle your category:

federal government   local government

education   family   environment

✎ Brainstorm and list what you may **want** in that category.

✎ Brainstorm and list what you may **need**.

WANTS	NEEDS

✎ Brainstorm and list what other people and organizations could provide for your needs. Tell how under "How to Provide."

OTHER PROVIDERS	HOW TO PROVIDE

✎ Brainstorm and list how you yourselves could provide for your needs.

SELF	HOW TO PROVIDE

26. Social-Political Literacy—
The Political Cartoon: No Laughing Matter

Acquiring Language Through . . . :   Pantomime, analyzing messages in political cartoons, and generating vocabulary.

Objective: To infer feelings and emotions from political cartoons.

Time Required: One class period.

Group Size: Four to six students.

Materials Needed: Reproducible 26 (one per group); five to seven political cartoons; large sentence strips or 5" by 8" index cards for flash cards.

Teaching Process

• **PREPARE**   Select several political cartoons from the newspaper. (Many Sunday papers provide a collection of the week's best in their opinion and editorial sections.) Use one cartoon for modeling. Paste each of the other cartoons onto one of the reproducibles. Prepare several flash cards. Write on them words with common expressions of emotions such as, *sad, happy, angry, evil, confused.*

• **INTRODUCE/MODEL**   In order to encourage second-language students to express feelings and points of view in English, give volunteers the flash cards you've prepared. Have them act out their word without telling or showing the others what's on the flash card. Have the other students guess the emotion. Write the words on chart paper and keep these as a word bank for this activity. If the students don't guess correctly, have the volunteers tell what they are miming.

Show an example of a political cartoon. Explain that political cartoons express feelings and emotions through picture clues. Ask for words to describe the facial expressions and actions happening in the pictures. Encourage less-proficient

students to refer to the word bank you've just established. Add new words to the word bank as they come up.

• **TEACH/PRACTICE**   Pass out the reproducibles with the pasted-on cartoons. Have students list at least five words in the circles on the reproducible that they see expressed in the cartoon.

Then ask students to work together to figure out what the cartoon means, based on their picture clues. Have them write a caption for it.

• **CONCLUDE/ASSESS**   Before you display the class's work, have each group make a tableau of their cartoon. (The tableau is a human sculpture, in which students freeze in a scene from the cartoon.) Ask the others to try to explain what they think the tableau of the cartoon means. Have a language-proficient student describe the tableau, while an early- or pre-production student acts it out. Then have a member of the group read their caption and share their word maps. Build your word bank with new words as they emerge.

Reproducible 26

The Political Cartoon: No Laughing Matter

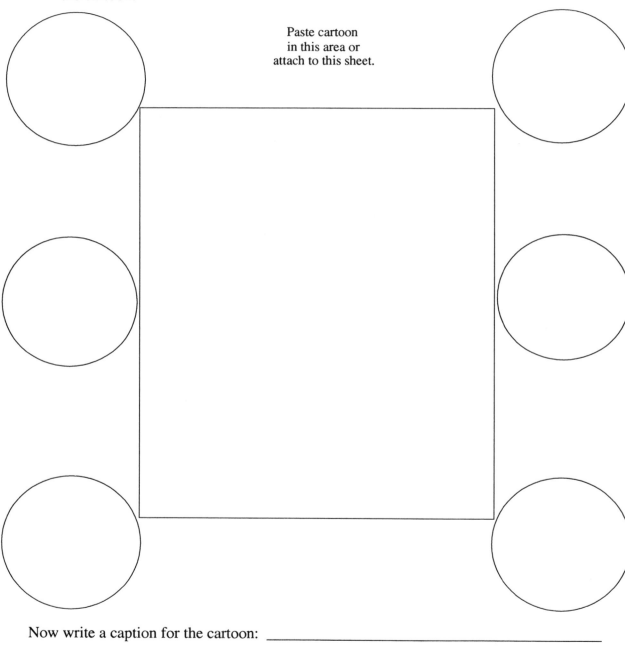

In the circles, list words to describe the emotions and feelings you see in the cartoon.

Paste cartoon
in this area or
attach to this sheet.

Now write a caption for the cartoon: _____

_____

27. Connecting to Literature—
Paul Revere's Ride

Acquiring Language Through . . . : poetry, discussion, mapping out a route, and pantomime.

Objective: Trace a route as described in a poem's words.

Time Required: One or more class periods.

Group Size: Four to five students.

Materials Needed: Reproducible 27A and 27B (one each per student); direction signs or flashcards; map of Boston/Lexington/Concord; tape recorder (optional); research resources on U.S. history of the Revolutionary War era.

Teaching Process

• **PREPARE**   Make an enlarged copy or an overhead transparency of Reproducible 27B.

Prepare direction signs replicating U.S. highway signs or use flash cards. Print on them the words **North, South, East, West.** Pre- and early-production students can benefit from assisting you while you review these words with them. Post your direction charts around the classroom. Be sure directions are true north, south, east, and west.

• **INTRODUCE/MODEL**   Revisit Activity 23 if you need to review cardinal direction. Show the cardinal directions on a classroom map of the United States or Massachusetts, and on the enlarged copy or overhead transparency of Reproducible 27B. Read "Paul Revere's Ride" aloud to the class. Trace the ride on the Reproducible 27B map. Repeat this with students as they say the directions of nearby reference points on the map. Point to the same directions in your classroom and name things that appear in those places. For background, you may wish to tell students about Paul Revere.

Paul Revere was an American patriot and skilled silversmith. He was born in Boston on January 1, 1735, and died on May 10, 1818. He is best remembered for his famous ride from Charlestown to Lexington, Massachusetts, on the night of April 18, 1775, to warn the countryside of advancing British troops. Revere arrived in Lexington and was soon joined by another rider, William Dawes. Their news allowed John Hancock and Benjamin Franklin to escape from Lexington before the British arrived. However, Revere was stopped by a British patrol on his way to Concord. Samuel Prescott was the patriot who actually reached Concord with the news.

• **TEACH/PRACTICE**   Reread the passages or record them so students can listen and read along independently. Have volunteers trace the journey on Reproducible 27B. Have the students point to and name other places of reference. Assign one section of the poem to each group to act out and map the route. Encourage them to use direction signs and cartoonlike drawings to illustrate the poem on the map.

• **CONCLUDE/ASSESS**   Have a student read the poem again to the class. Have each group show their illustrated map for their section. Assess how the illustrations support the reading. With a little bit of encouragement and lots of laughter, your students might pantomime or choreograph movement to the reading. As an extra, optional activity, have each group research the actual historical facts about their section of the poem. Have groups present their findings orally to the class. If you prefer, you could present the real facts yourself.

Paul Revere's Ride

✎ Read the section of the poem your teacher has assigned to your group. On Reproducible 27B, trace the part of Paul Reveres' route in your section of the poem. Plan how to act it out to the class.

Paul Revere's Ride (an excerpt)

by Henry Wadsworth Longfellow

1. Listen, my children, and you shall hear
   Of the midnight ride of Paul Revere,
   On the eighteenth of April, in Seventy-five;
   Hardly a man is now alive
   Who remembers that famous day and year.

2. He said to his friend, "If the British march
   By land or sea from the town to-night,
   Hang a lantern aloft in the belfry arch
   Of the North Church tower as a signal light,—
   One, if by land, and two, if by sea;
   And I on the opposite shore will be,
   Ready to ride and spread the alarm
   Through every Middlesex village and farm,
   For the country-folk to up and to arm."

3. Then he said, "Good night!" and with muffled oar
   Silently rowed to the Charlestown shore,
   Just as the moon rose over the bay. . . .

4. . . . On the opposite shore walked Paul Revere. . .
   He springs to the saddle, the bridle he turns,. . .
   He has left the village and mounted the steep,
   And beneath him, tranquil and broad and deep,
   Is the Mystic, meeting the ocean tides. . . .

5. It was twelve by the village clock,
   When he crossed the bridge into Medford town.

6. It was one by the village clock,
   When he galloped into Lexington.

7. It was two by the village clock,
   When he came to the bridge in Concord town.
   He heard the bleating of the flock,
   And the twitter of birds among the trees,
   And felt the breath of the morning breeze
   Blowing over the meadows brown.

8. So through the night rode Paul Revere:
   And so through the night went his cry of alarm
   To every Middlesex village and farm,
   A cry of defiance and not of fear,
   A voice in the darkness, a knock at the door,
   And a word that shall echo forevermore!

Paul Revere's Ride

✎ Trace the part of Paul Revere's route in your section of the poem. Plan how to act it out to the class.

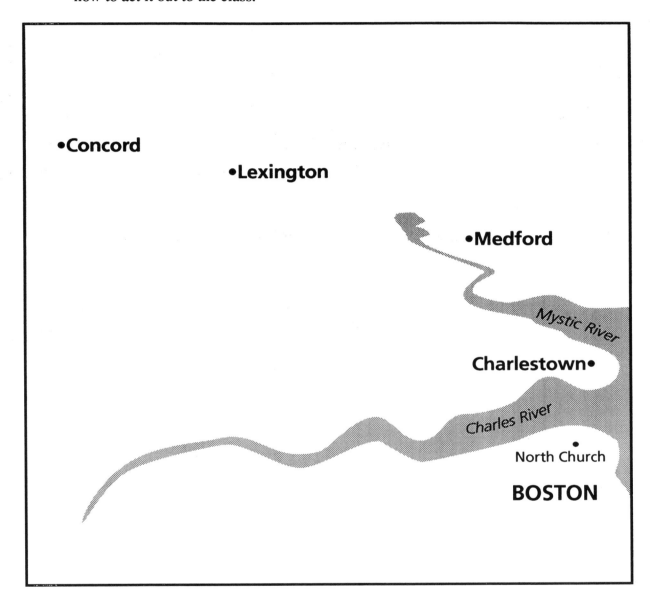

✎ **Optional:** Longfellow's famous poem does not fit the actual facts from history about Paul Revere's ride. Research the real facts about your section of the poem, and report them orally to the class.

28. Connecting to Literature—
The Gettysburg Address

Acquiring Language Through . . . : Choral reading and pattern responses, and the jigsaw cooperative learning strategy.

Objective: To familiarize students with the Gettysburg Address.

Time Required: Two to three class periods—one or two to introduce and work with expert groups, one to work with home groups.

Group Size: Six equal groups.

Materials Needed: Reproducible 28 (one per student); six audiotapes.

Teaching Process

• **PREPARE** Record the Gettysburg Address in its entirety on audiotape. (A student from the drama department is always willing to do this.) Then dub five consecutive sections of the address on five individual tapes; see the numbered sections on the reproducible. (This eliminates the need to cue the tape continually.)

• **INTRODUCE/MODEL** Introduce the Gettysburg Address by familiarizing the students with Abraham Lincoln. Show the students a Lincoln penny or display a picture of Lincoln. For background, you may wish to tell students that Lincoln gave this address on November 19, 1863, at the site of the Civil War Battle of Gettysburg in Pennsylvania. The speech was given as part of the dedication of the Gettysburg cemetery.

• **TEACH/PRACTICE** Teach the Gettysburg Address, breaking it into pieces, or making a "jigsaw" of it. (The following strategy is based on configuring five groups with five students each. You may have fewer students, so adapt and recalculate the configuration accordingly.)

1. Divide students into five home groups: A, B, C, D, E.

2. Number each person in the group: 1, 2, 3, 4, 5.

3. All the 1's, 2's, 3's, 4's, and 5's reassemble into groups according to their numbers. These are known as "expert groups."

4. Have students in each expert group read along as they listen to their section of the Gettysburg Address. Then have them decide how they might teach or explain their section of the address once they reconvene in their home groups.

5. Have each home group (A–E) reconvene and have each expert (1–5) teach his or her section to the group.

• **CONCLUDE/ASSESS** Create a word bank of all unfamiliar words. Have each expert group commit their section to memory, and then group by group, give a choral reading of the address.

The Gettysburg Address

✎ In your expert group, read along while listening to the section of the Gettysburg address your teacher has assigned to your group. Plan how to teach your section to your home group. You can make a poster using words and drawings to describe your section. Or you can play your section on tape and tell its meaning in your own words. Or you can act out your section by presenting a skit.

1. Fourscore and seven years ago our fathers brought forth on this continent a new nation, conceived in liberty and dedicated to the proposition that all men are created equal.

2. Now we are engaged in a great civil war, testing whether that nation or any nation so conceived and so dedicated can long endure. We are met on a great battlefield of that war. We have come to dedicate a portion of that field as a final resting-place for those who here gave their lives that that nation might live. It is altogether fitting and proper that we should do this.

3. But in a larger sense, we cannot dedicate—we cannot consecrate—we cannot hallow—this ground. The brave men, living and dead, who struggled here, have consecrated it, far above our poor power to add or detract.

4. The world will little note nor long remember what we say here, but it can never forget what they did here. It is for us the living, rather, to be dedicated here to the unfinished work which they who fought here have thus far so nobly advanced.

5. It is rather for us to be here dedicated to the great task remaining before us—that from these honored dead we take increased devotion to that cause for which they gave the last full measure of devotion—that we here highly resolve that these dead shall not have died in vain—that this nation under God shall have a new birth of freedom—and that government of the people, by the people, for the people, shall not perish from the earth.

61

29. Together at School— Think/Pair/Share

Acquiring Language Through . . . : Discussion, the media, and generating vocabulary.

Objectives: To foster communicating in English with peers; to provide examples of pro-social behavior.

Time Required: One class period.

Group Size: Pairs followed by even-numbered groups of four to six students.

Materials Needed: Reproducible 29 (one per pair); magazines, newspapers, postcards; scissors; tape or paste.

Teaching Process

- **PREPARE** Cut out pictures of people enjoying themselves as they participate in healthful, fun activities. Help your early-production students identify the activities. They might be anything from sports to dancing, or just relaxing. This should be an extensive picture file, since sometimes different students will want to picture the same activity.

- **INTRODUCE/MODEL** Introduce students to the process for this activity by writing on the chalkboard: *think, pair,* and *share*. Shelter the instruction by exaggerating your gestures and facial expressions as you explain first, thinking, then talking in pairs, then sharing.

  Tell students that they should first **think** about what they do or should do to keep their minds and bodies healthy. Model this by describing ways that you personally stay fit, stay healthy, and just stay sane—which may be something as ambitious as a gym regimen or as comforting as talking to another teacher about some problem.

Give them some time to talk this over in **pairs**. Encourage fluent speakers to ask questions of early-production students as if they were interviewing them.

Then have the pairs work in groups to **share** their ideas. Assign a group recorder to chart responses. Finally, have each group share their responses with the class. List all the responses on chart paper and keep as a word bank.

- **TEACH/PRACTICE** Distribute Reproducible 29. Make sure students understand the directions. Have the students work again in partners and then in groups to complete the reproducible, this time selecting pictures to show their responses.

- **CONCLUDE/ASSESS** Refer to your word bank. Poll your students about their favorite activities. Tally the results on the word bank. Pre- and early-production students might be the counters as you poll the class activity by activity.

Think / Pair / Share

THINK: What do you do to keep fit and stay well—both body and mind? _____

PAIR: Partner 1 _____

_____

_____

Partner 2 _____

_____

_____

SHARE: Tape or paste pictures of what you do in the space below to share with the class.

30. Promoting Participation—
Have You Got a Problem with That?

Acquiring Language Through . . . : Discussion, reading, and using realia (newspapers, phone books).

Objectives: To use the phone book; to practice participation skills.

Time Required: Two class periods.

Group Size: Four to six students.

Materials Needed: Reproducible 30 (one per group); telephone yellow and blue pages (one per group); newspaper articles, videotape highlights of news broadcasts.

Teaching Process

• **PREPARE** Collect phone books.

Thumb through newspapers, particularly the metro sections, to find recent articles on local city and community problems. You might also tape news broadcasts featuring such problems. On the chalkboard, create two columns—one headed ***Problems***, the other headed ***Solutions***.

• **INTRODUCE/MODEL** Explain that the quality of life in a community is sometimes threatened by problems. To support this, showcase recent news articles or videotapes of news broadcasts featuring local problems. Identify them and list them in the ***Problems*** column.

Then tell the class that one way to find solutions to a community problem is to use the phone book. Encourage early-production students to thumb through several phone books in order to get a sense of the information. Identify the table of contents, icons, yellow and blue pages, and easy reference lists for government and other public services.

Model this for students by taking an issue such as homelessness and looking up listings where one could get referrals, such as the public welfare department or family and children's services, List such information under **Solutions**.

• **TEACH/PRACTICE** As a class, brainstorm and list community problems based on your readings and discussions. Have each group choose at least one problem. Have them analyze the problem and find possible people, agencies, and services in the phone book that can assist in solving the problem. Provide each group with a phone book.

Have students use Reproducible 30 to organize their work. After you distribute it, make sure they understand the directions.

• **CONCLUDE/ASSESS** Collect all the information from the groups. As a class, review the findings, interpret them, and correct them as necessary. You may wish to put this together as a resource book. The book itself can then become part of a class portfolio that you can use for assessment.

You could also have students discuss ways in which they personally can be part of the solution.

Group Names _____

Date _____

Have You Got a Problem with That?

 Brainstorm community problems. Choose one to investigate as a group.

Find a person, agency, or service in the telephone book able to help solve the problem.

Then note how the person/organization can help be part of the solution.

PROBLEMS	SOLUTIONS
	Name of Person /Organization: _____ _____ _____ _____ _____ **Address:** _____ _____ _____ _____ **Phone Number:** _____ _____ **Type of Help:** _____ _____ _____ _____ _____ _____

31. Working Together in the Workplace— Who Works for You?

Acquiring Language Through . . . : Using realia, analyzing local maps, and generating vocabulary.

Objectives: To provide examples of career and vocational opportunities; to foster appreciation for work.

Time Required: Two class periods—one to introduce and teach, one to conclude.

Group Size: Six equal groups.

Materials Needed: Reproducible 31 (one per group); promotional materials about your city, town, or region; materials for job reference such as classified and business sections from newspapers, encyclopedias, printouts from job banks and employment offices, telephone yellow and blue pages; an illustrated city map and, optionally, the map and mural made in Activity 24, "City, Town, All Around."

Teaching Process

- **PREPARE** On the chalkboard or on individual sheets of chart paper, write the following categories: *food, clothing, shelter, family, school, well-being.* Display local maps and job reference materials.

- **INTRODUCE/MODEL** Begin with a general discussion of what makes the place where you live a good place to live or what could make it better. To organize your discussion, brainstorm the categories listed on the chalkboard or chart paper. Develop pattern questions, such as:

  "Where do you go in your community for food (clothing, shelter)? "
  "What jobs/work provide food (clothing, shelter)? "
  "What jobs/work help your family (school, well-being)?"

  Have pre- and early-production students use the brochures and realia to show their responses. List several responses before you break up into groups. (There will be duplications.)

- **TEACH/PRACTICE** Distribute Reproducible 31. Go over any questions students may have about completing the work. Facilitate the group work as necessary.

  When all groups have completed the reproducible, assemble the class and combine the lists.

- **CONCLUDE/ASSESS** Assign a category from the reproducible to each group. Have each group select one or two jobs from their category to research using the job reference materials you've provided and also consulting the Internet and the career and vocational office at school.

  Conclude by having the students role-play a work situation, give a short presentation in the form of a business management report, or create a poster or collage describing jobs and careers available in your community.

Reproducible 31

Who Works for You?

 List the jobs necessary to provide you with food, clothing, and shelter.

FOOD	CLOTHING	SHELTER

 List the jobs and careers that assist your family, school, and well-being.

FAMILY	SCHOOL	WELL-BEING

32. Resolving Conflict Creatively—
There's Something I Want to Get Clear Here

Acquiring Language Through . . . : Active listening, conversation, and generating vocabulary.

Objective: To analyze values and opinions.

Time Required: One class period to introduce the activity. The game outlined in the activity can take several periods to play.

Group Size: Partners and then groups of five to eight students.

Materials Needed: Reproducible 32 (one per group); a CD; card stock.

Teaching Process

- **PREPARE** Prepare Reproducible 32 on card stock (one copy per group). Cut along the lines to make cards.

- **INTRODUCE/MODEL** Hold up a CD in front of the class and ask the following question. "Suppose you and a friend were in a music store. After you've left the store, your friend shows you a CD he or she has shoplifted." (Explain the term shoplifted to the limited-English students.) "What would you do?" Discuss and share students responses.Would students report the theft to the store? to some other adults? Would they insist that their friend return the CD? Would they tell their friend that shoplifting is wrong and it is also illegal? Would they say nothing? (If language production is not high, you might suggest some of these responses.)

  Write the following idiom on the chalkboard: "Everything's not black or white." You may need to explain to newcomers what an idiom is before you discuss the meaning of what you wrote.

  Help students understand that every day we encounter situations that are difficult, that test our values. Invite language-proficient students to share situations from their own lives where they've encountered dilemmas similar to the CD-shoplifting incident, where things aren't black or white.

- **TEACH/PRACTICE** Explain that the class will play a game in which they'll ask themselves, "What do I think?" "What do I feel?" Using the shoplifting example, practice the statements, "I think . . ." and "I feel . . ." Select students who need practice to finish the statements. Arrange each group of students in a circle, seated in chairs, at desks, or on the floor. Pass out a set of cards to each group. Establish the following rules.

  Ground Rules:
  1. One person speaks at a time.
  2. Students always have a right to pass.
  3. Explain that what they say is confidential; whatever is said in the group/class stays in the group/class.

  Directions:
  1. Place a stack of cards in the middle of each group circle.
  2. Have each person pick a card in turn and read it aloud. Have more fluent English readers help the early- and intermediate-production learners.
  3. Ask each person, in turn, to respond to his or her card, beginning responses with "I think . . ." and/or "I feel . . ." (Sometimes you may need to encourage pre- and early-production students who may only be able to sit by and listen.)

**32. Resolving Conflict Creatively—
There's Something I Want to
Get Clear Here** *(continued)*

Teacher
Guide
Page

4. Once the student has responded, others may ask a question or make a comment only by raising a hand and being recognized by the person holding the floor.

• **CONCLUDE/ASSESS**   Keep an idea box in the classroom. Label it *What do I think about . . .?/ What do I feel about. . .?* Encourage students to design their own questions and put them in the box.

Challenge students to write their problems concerning growing up or their questions about morals and values on cards and put them in the box. Once you have a number of cards, you can use this activity at any time to reward students for their work or to provide active listening and directed speaking opportunities.

There's Something I Want to Get Clear Here

Teacher's Directions: Enlarge, copy, and cut cards along the lines. Be sure to include some cards with problems and situations relevant to your class.

How would you change the world if you could?	What are your hopes, dreams, and goals for the future?
What makes a perfect father?	When should you be treated like a grown-up?
If you had three wishes, what would they be?	Describe the perfect teacher.
What kind of person would make a perfect relationship for you?	If you or a friend had trouble, would you call the police? Why or why not?
What makes up the best kind of family?	If you were a parent, what would you want for your child?
Discuss divorce.	What would you do if you won a million dollars in the lottery?
What are the best qualities in a friend?	Describe the perfect mother.

33. Resolving Conflicts Creatively—
Random Acts of Kindness

Acquiring Language Through . . . : Generating vocabulary through discussion, and writing and drawing descriptions.

Objectives: To write simple sentences using *who*, *what*, *where*, *when*, *why*, and *how*; to enhance self-esteem through peer interaction.

Time Required: Three class periods—one to introduce and model, one to teach and practice designing the random acts of kindness, one to conclude through sharing and follow-up. (Note: Nonclassroom time is necessary for this activity.)

Group Size: Four to six students.

Materials Needed: Reproducible 33 (one per student); a variety of motivational rewards and incentives.

Teacher-to-Teacher: Many of our ESL students have been treated differently by their peers. Some have been lucky and have made friends quickly, and others have had a tough time. This activity allows ESL and language-proficient students to interact.

Teaching Process

• **PREPARE** Gather together prizes or treats and plan some fun and amusing incentives, such as five minutes of extra free time, smiling a lot, giving lots of praise, even giving out jelly beans. These will be your unexpected random acts of kindness to reward your students. Ask your students for their own suggestions.

• **INTRODUCE/MODEL** Begin the class by performing your random acts of kindness. Have students brainstorm how it felt to be the recipient of your kindness. Help students review emotional descriptors, such as happy and sad (see Activity 26). Brainstorm words students associate with such words as *surprised*, *respected*, and *appreciated*. Add new words to the class word bank.

Brainstorm acts of kindness that students could practice with friends, classmates, family members, and neighbors. Prompt them, referring to your own actions that started the class and modeling other acts you've done or others have done to you.

Write the words *who*, *what*, *where*, *when*, *why*, and *how* on the chalkboard. After you have a list of

actions, have students discuss how to complete the acts of kindness. Break up the tasks by asking questions about them using the words you've written on the board.

• **TEACH/PRACTICE** Pass out copies of Reproducible 33 (one to each student). As students work in groups, ask them to think about ways to reach out and be kind to someone at school, at home, or in the neighborhood. They can use one or more of the ideas they brainstormed, or they can extend the idea list. They should use a separate reproducible for each act of kindness.

Instruct students to keep a sense of surprise about the activities. Encourage and facilitate whatever individual needs students may have to complete their random acts of kindness.

• **CONCLUDE/ASSESS** Provide an opportunity for students to tell about their actions, offer feedback, and ask questions. Collect the reproducible together in a class book and make a copy for each student. This can be their reminder to practice random acts of kindness whenever possible.

Group Names ______________________________

Date ______________________________

Reproducible 33

Random Acts of Kindness

Think about your random act of kindness. Describe it. Sketch it here.

Describe it here.

Who? ______________________________

What? ______________________________

Where? ______________________________

When? ______________________________

Why? ______________________________

How? ______________________________

34. Resolving Conflicts Creatively—
When the Pressure's On

Acquiring Language Through . . . :   Role-playing, active listening, and following a procedure.

Objective: To express feelings and opinions; to practice refusal skills.

Time Required :   One class period.

Group Size: Four to six students.

Materials Needed: Reproducible 34 (one per group); sentence strips or flash cards.

Teaching Process

• **PREPARE**   Write each of the refusal skills listed on Reproducible 34 on its own flash card.

• **INTRODUCE/MODEL**   Explain that there are ways to get out of a situation other than just saying no. Use examples from your own life. Shelter the instruction by pantomiming and having volunteers act out that situation with you.

Display the flash cards that show refusal skills. Point to individual refusal skills. Make sure students understand each skill by having the inter-mediate and fluent students talk about them, while early-production students act them out. For example, brainstorm ways someone may avoid a risk behavior by walking away or changing the subject. List examples. Challenge students to be specific. Have them act out a scene, such as one kid offering

another a cigarette or beer. Model conversations such as saying, "Look, there's Rashid. I have to go." or "My little sister needs me."

• **TEACH/PRACTICE**   Ask each group to use Reproducible 34 as a reference. Have them brain-storm, role-play, and list scenarios of risk behaviors (where and when they need to use refusal skills). Then have them brainstorm, role-play, and list the appropriate refusal skill(s) to get out of a situation that puts them at risk (how to do it). Have them record (in words or pictures) a scenario for each refusal skill on the reproducible.

• **CONCLUDE/ASSESS**   As a class, have each group act out their scenarios. Have the class guess which refusal skill(s) the group is using. Discuss the benefits and/or implications of using such techniques.

When the Pressure's On

Describe in words or pictures a situation in which you use each of these refusal skills.

Walk away.	Ignore the person.
Change the subject.	Keep saying no.
Avoid the situation.	Say, "No thanks."
Give a reason.	There's strength in numbers. Go in groups.

Make up an excuse.

35. Resolving Conflict Creatively—
One Thing that Really Gets Me Mad

Acquiring Language Through . . . :   Conversation, practice repetition, and generating vocabulary.

Objectives: To foster social-political awareness; to analyze responses to anger.

Time Required: One class period.

Group Size: Partners, then groups of four to six students.

Materials Needed: Reproducible 35 (one per group).

Teaching Process

• **PREPARE**   Simply make copies of the reproducible and proceed with the activity.

• **INTRODUCE/MODEL**   Invite students to show what they do when they get angry. Write on the chalkboard: **Who/What? When? How?**

Prompt students by asking them: "Who or what got you angry?" "When did you get angry?" "What took place?" "How was it resolved?"

Have the students work in pairs to discuss the questions. Reconvene and have the students describe what happened. Write as many responses on the chalkboard as you can.

Help students see that in some instances their anger was constructive, that it was necessary. Other times it hurt them; it was destructive. Model this by giving your own experiences and opinions.

• **TEACH/PRACTICE**   Distribute Reproducible 35. Make sure students understand the instructions. Point out that instead of looking at instances in their own lives, they are to look at problems in the world around them that make them angry and analyze these in the way you modeled. Before students break up into groups, you may want to model a problem, such as racism.

• **CONCLUDE/ASSESS**   Create a word web with *anger* in the middle. Have the students contribute their examples from group work of things that make them angry. Record their responses on the web. Discuss examples of people who have made a difference by being angry and doing something constructive about it (e.g., Martin Luther King, Jr., Cesar Chavez, Susan B. Anthony).

Reproducible 35

One Thing that Really Gets Me Mad

What really gets you mad in the world around you? List at least three things. For each, tell who or what gets you really mad, when you got/get angry, and how you have dealt with your anger, or how the situation was resolved.

Analyze the following:

W Who/What?	W When?	H How?

— What would make it worse? | + What would make it better?

61 Cooperative Learning Activities in ESL

III. THINKING AND COMMUNICATING IN MATH

36. Thinking with Math—
Walking the Line

Acquiring Language Through . . . : Total physical response, pantomime, and generating math statements.

Objective: To create mathematical statements using positive and negative integers.

Time Required: One class period.

Group Size: Four students.

Materials Needed: Reproducible 36; two different colored number cubes (dice) (one set per group); index cards.

Teaching Process

• **PREPARE** Make a number line on a six-foot sheet of butcher paper. Label it from –36 to +36. Place it on the floor where their is room to see it and stand on it. (You may also do this activity outdoors, writing the number line with chalk on the blacktop.) Supply two number cubes in two different colors for each group.

• **INTRODUCE/MODEL** Write the words *positive* and *negative* on the chalkboard. Brainstorm what the words mean. List the meanings. Make the transition to math by stating that in this activity, students will work with positive and negative numbers. Assign a die of one color for negative integers and a die of another color for positive integers. Roll each cube and record the numbers. Demonstrate how to construct an addition sentence from those numbers. For example, if you rolled a 3 on the positive cube and a 4 on the negative cube, your sentence reads: +3 + –4 = –1.

Show this on the number line with an index card marker, or have students stand on –1. Roll the cubes several more times, helping students as they build addition sentences. Then demonstrate rolling the cubes and making sentences for subtraction, multiplication, and division. Use this as a point of entry to increase vocabulary. Make a game of assigning objects to the mathematical sentences. For example:

+3 notebooks + –4 notebooks = –1 notebook

As you demonstrate, show students how to fill in the information on Reproducible 36 (see example below).

• **TEACH/PRACTICE** Distribute Reproducible 36 and make sure the students understand the instructions. Encourage pre- or early-production students to roll the cubes, say the numbers, and repeat the math sentence.

• **CONCLUDE/ASSESS** Have each group act out their sentence on the number line. Use this opportunity to asses how second-language students are using numbers and building vocabulary.

+ positive number	– negative number	mathematical sentence
+3	–4	+3 notebooks + –4 notebooks = –1 notebook

Group Names _____

Date _____

Walking the Line

✎ Roll the die. Record the numbers.

✎ Write mathematical sentences on the line provided. Insert a word after each number in your equation. Remember the rule: You can't add apples and oranges!

✎ Select your best sentence. Pantomime, act out, or make a line dance to demonstrate your equation. See if the rest of the class can guess your mathematical sentence.

	+ positive number	– negative number	mathematical sentence
1. addition			_____ _____ _____ _____ _____
2. subtraction			_____ _____ _____ _____ _____
3. multiplication			_____ _____ _____ _____ _____
4. division			_____ _____ _____ _____ _____

37. Thinking with Math—
Rate It! Time It!

Acquiring Language Through . . . : Using manipulatives and investigating.

Objective: To calculate rate and time.

Time Required: One class period.

Group Size: Three to four students.

Materials Needed: Reproducible 37 (one per student); two to three large bags of M&Ms™ (you may use beans, but they're not as much fun); coffee can or take-out food container with plastic cover (one per group); paper cups; a watch with a second hand.

Teaching Process

• **PREPARE** Divide several packages of M&Ms into paper cups. You may wish to make a trial run of this activity in order to estimate how much candy you'll need.

Supply a coffee can or similar container for each group. Cut a hole in the lid of each container, large enough to fit one candy through.

• **INTRODUCE/MODEL** Start with a general discussion. Ask the class if they've ever thought about how long it takes them to complete a task such as cleaning their room, mowing the lawn, or doing their math homework. Explain that this activity will give them the tools to measure the time it takes to perform a task.

• **TEACH/PRACTICE** Explain the task. Set only one rule: The cups of M&Ms and the containers must stay in place. Give each group two minutes to figure out how their group will fill the container, moving one M&M at a time to the container. Students must determine *who* will do it, *how* to do it, and *who* will be the counter. Then give them one minute to complete the task. Encourage all group methods for completing the task.

Ask an early- or intermediate-language learner in each group to count the number of

M&Ms in the container and record the number on Reproducible 37 under "1 minute."

Write *r/t* on the chalkboard. Ask students what this means. Show them that r = the number of M&Ms in the container; t = 1 minute. Rewrite the formula using the students' results—for example, 20 (M&Ms) / 1 (minute). Explain that the number of M&Ms in a container is the **rate per minute**.

Have the students determine how many M&Ms would be in the container if they continued to fill for 3 minutes. Ask them to explain how they figured this out.

Write $r \times t = n$ on the chalkboard. Using the example of 20 M&Ms in a container after 1 minute, in 3 minutes there would be 3 times 20, or 60 M&Ms: $r \times t = n$, or $20 \times 3 = 60$ M&Ms.

Ask students to record their responses for 3, 4, and 5 minutes on Reproducible 37. Then, have them complete the reproducible.

• **CONCLUDE/ASSESS** Assess language acquisition and problem solving by discussing Part 2 of the reproducible with each group. Share the more creative solutions with the class. Allow the students to "eat the evidence," in which case you could lead a discussion of negative numbers.

Rate It! Time It!

 Part 1. How many M&Ms fill the cup?

$$r \times t = n$$

1 minute	3 minutes	4 minutes	5 minutes

 Part 2. Choose one of the following problems. Explain how you might compute the answer by using rate × time. Use your own words.

• There are many, many things in your locker. How long will it take to clean the locker?

_____

_____

_____

_____

_____

• You must deliver seven pizzas in one hour. How many minutes do you have to deliver each pizza?

_____

_____

_____

_____

_____

• How long does it take a class member on the track team to run a mile? How long would she or he take to run a 5-miler?

_____

_____

_____

38. Using Math—
The Price Is Right

Acquiring Language Through . . . : Collage, decision-making, and discussion.

Objective: To use addition, subtraction, and multiplication to solve consumer math problems.

Time Required: One class period.

Group Size: Partners.

Materials Needed: Reproducible 38 (one per group); grocery advertisements from local newspapers, coupon books, and circulars; scissors; glue or tape; poster board.

Teaching Process

• **PREPARE** Collect several grocery advertisements with prices clearly marked. Cut out pictures of a few grocery items along with their prices, and glue or tape them to poster board.

• **INTRODUCE/MODEL** Display your collage of two or three grocery items with the prices clearly marked. Point to each grocery item. Have students identify it by name, and state the price.

Write down each price on the chalkboard. Share how you shop for food, telling how many people are in your family and how you add or multiply prices depending on the amount of different items you have to purchase.

• **TEACH/PRACTICE** Pass out Reproducible 38. Model item 1 on the reproducible. Have students work in pairs, one language-proficient and one pre- or early-production student. Have students list five grocery items that each partner might buy. Once they have done this, pass out a variety of grocery advertisements. Have students find the grocery items that they listed and write the prices for those items on the reproducible. Remind each pair how you had to allow for the members of your family when you did your calculations and that they need to do the same. Show them how to multiply or

add their individual prices to get a total price for each item. Then have each pair add up both lists to find the two *sums*.

Once everyone has totaled their grocery lists, have them figure the *difference* between the two amounts spent by each partner. Show them how to subtract the smaller amount from the larger number to get the difference.

Have students glue or tape the pictures of their items to poster board to create a collage.

• **CONCLUDE/ASSESS** After everyone has completed their collages and calculations, bring all the students back together as a whole group and ask for volunteers to share their findings and display their groups' collage.

Then, have students cut their collages apart into individual items. Put all of them into a box and ask your pre- or early-production learners to hold up the pictures one by one as students call out the names and prices of the grocery items.

Have a more fluent English speaker record on chart paper the names of the items as they are said and then tape each picture next to its name to develop a word-picture bank for the classroom wall.

The Price is Right

1. List five grocery items that you and that your partner might buy.

2. Using grocery ads, find the price per item. Write the price next to each item in the column labeled "Individual Price."

3. Decide how much you'd buy of each item for your family. Then figure the total cost of the item. Write this in the column labeled "Total Cost."

4. Find the **sum**, or total, of all the "Total Cost" figures in each column. Write this on the "Sum" lines.

5. Figure the **difference** between the two sums (subtract the smaller number from the larger one). Write this on the "Difference" line.

Partner #1 Number in Family _____   **Partner #2 Number in Family _____**

Item	Individual Price	Total Cost	Item	Individual Price	Total Cost
1._____	_____	_____	1._____	_____	_____
2._____	_____	_____	2._____	_____	_____
3._____	_____	_____	3._____	_____	_____
4._____	_____	_____	4._____	_____	_____
5._____	_____	_____	5._____	_____	_____

Sum:_____   Sum:_____

Difference:_____

39. Using Math—
How Do We Measure Up?

Acquiring Language Through . . . : Using manipulatives and comparison.

Objective: To learn and practice the terms *centimeter, millimeter, measure,* and *ruler.*

Time Required: One class period.

Group Size: Four students.

Materials Needed: Reproducible 39 (one per group); several packages of miniature marshmallows; paper cups (one per group); bamboo skewers (one per group); metric rulers (one per group); small classroom items (pencils, folders, textbooks, etc.).

Teaching Process

• **PREPARE** Fill one paper cup with miniature marshmallows for each group. Fill a skewer with miniature marshmallows. Do not allow any space between marshmallows.

Select or collect various classroom items for students to measure.

Prepare an overhead of Reproducible 39 or write a facsimile on the chalkboard.

• **INTRODUCE/MODEL** Refer to the transparency of Reproducible 39. Explain that students will measure things with marshmallows. Model measuring one item by holding the skewer alongside the item and counting marshmallows.

• **TEACH/PRACTICE** Have students work in groups to load skewers with marshmallows. Review safety rules. Distribute Reproducible 39. Make sure students understand directions.

Have students measure several items and list their measurements on Reproducible 39. Have groups be sure to verify the count of marshmallows before listing the totals.

Have each group share their findings with the whole class. Discussion should center on looking at why the amounts are all different. (Each miniature marshmallow is slightly different in size, and therefore not an accurate measure.)

• **CONCLUDE/ASSESS** Have the students measure their items again, but this time using the metric rulers. Have them measure the item, first in centimeters and then in millimeters, and record their findings on Reproducible 39. Compare the groups' measurements with one another.

How Do We Measure Up?

✎ Measure five items.

✎ First measure with marshmallows. Report your group findings to the class.

✎ Then measure with a standard metric ruler.

MARSHMALLOW MEASURE

Item	Measurement (number of marshmallows)
1. _____	_____
2. _____	_____
3. _____	_____
4. _____	_____
5. _____	_____

STANDARD MEASURE

Item	Measurement	
	centimeters	millimeters
1. _____		
2. _____		
3. _____		
4. _____		
5. _____		

40. Using Math— Dollars and Cents

Acquiring Language Through . . . : Total physical response.

Objective: To learn the terms *dollars, cents, decimal point,* and use them in consumer situations.

Time Required: One class period.

Group Size: Five equal groups of students.

Materials Needed: Reproducible 40 (one per group); 3" by 5" index cards; real or play money, representing U.S. currency; a variety of mail-order catalogs, supermarket flyers, and advertising supplements.

Teaching Process

• **PREPARE** Prepare four to six number cards for each group. Write a different two-digit number from 10 to 99 on each card. Gather a variety of mail-order catalogs and advertising supplements. Separate them into categories of food, clothing, automotive, housewares, and electronics.

Write the words **dollars** and **cents** on the chalkboard.

• **INTRODUCE/MODEL** Invite two early-production students to help you introduce money expressions to the class. Give each volunteer a number card. Have them say their number. Ask one to write his or her number under *dollars* and other to write the number under *cents*. Draw a big dollar sign to the left of the first number and a big decimal point between the numbers to indicate dollars and cents. Read the new expression aloud with the class. (For example, 45 and 52 is expressed as "forty-five dollars and fifty-two cents.")

• **TEACH/PRACTICE** Display a variety of currency. Point out that all paper denominations go on the *dollars* side. All coins (except Susan B. Anthony coins) go on the *cents* side. Practice as necessary.

Pass out copies of Reproducible 40 and an even amount of number cards (18 to 20). Make sure students understand the directions. Challenge them to go on a shopping spree. Assign a different consumer category to each group with corresponding catalogues. Instruct them to use individual amounts to purchase individual items or use sums of the individual amounts to purchase more expensive items. As necessary, work with individual ESL students to practice expressing items in dollars and cents.

• **CONCLUDE/ASSESS** Have students tell what each of their groups bought. List these on chart paper as part of a word bank, and use the word bank to generate vocabulary of everyday items. Assess ESL students' facility with expressing terms in dollars and cents.

Reproducible 40

Dollars and Cents

✎ Divide your number cards into two piles. List the numbers in the first pile under **dollars.** List the numbers in the second pile under **cents.** Draw a decimal point and read the new amount aloud to the group.

DOLLARS	CENTS		DOLLARS	CENTS

✎ What would you like to buy? Use the amounts from above—individual amounts or sums of several individual amounts. Go through the catalog and price lists to find items you can buy with the money listed above.

Category _____

Item _____   Price _____

Total _____

41. Using Math— Trains, Planes, and Transit Trips

Acquiring Language Through . . . : Reading charts/timetables and research.

Objectives: To use a timetable; to estimate and calculate time elapsed.

Time Required: One to two class periods.

Group Size: Two to four students.

Materials Needed: Reproducible 41 (one per student); bus, train, flight, or other transit schedules and transit maps (a set for each group); world map (optional); analog clock or watch with movable hands (one per group).

Teaching Process

• **PREPARE** Collect transit and travel schedules from your local transit authority, bus or train station, and travel agent. Prepare an overhead of a timetable.

• **INTRODUCE/MODEL** Referring to the overhead, show how to estimate elapsed travel time. You might display a clock and turn the clock ahead, asking students to tell each interval of time. Point out additional transit and travel information, such as express stops, A.M. or P.M. service, arrival, departure, and various abbreviations.

• **TEACH/PRACTICE** Distribute Reproducible 41 and a transit schedule and map for each group.

Make sure students understand the directions. Facilitate the group work, as each group selects three excursions to figure for elapsed time. Help early-production students locate each stop on a local timetable and point to it on the map.

• **CONCLUDE/ASSESS** After students calculate their elapsed travel time from home to school, have them create a classroom bar graph using a variety of measurements, such as individual elapsed time; average elapsed time of the group; elapsed time walking, running, biking, and/or riding on the bus or in the car. Use this activity to assess how well your limited-English students tell time in English.

Trains, Planes, and Transit Trips

🖉 Work together in groups. Look at the schedule provided. Find the elapsed time for three or more trips. Draw the hands of the clocks for the start and the finish of each trip, and calculate the elapsed time.

Start   Finish

Elapsed time: _____

Start   Finish

Elapsed time: _____

Start   Finish

Elapsed time: _____

🖉 Now, Find the elapsed time of your trip from home to school. Draw the hands of the clocks for the start and finish and calculate the elapsed time.

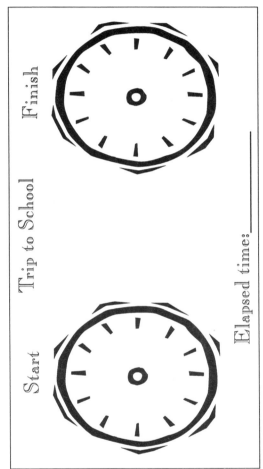

Trip to School

Start   Finish

Elapsed time: _____

42. Using Math—
The Cost of Addiction

Acquiring Language Through . . . : Total physical response and using print realia.

Objective: To calculate the cost of cigarette smoking.

Time Required: Two to three class periods.

Group Size: Four to six students.

Materials Needed: Reproducible 42 (one per group); a variety of travel-related print materials; scissors; tape or glue; marking pens; poster board.

Teaching process

• **PREPARE** Collect a variety of travel-related materials: newspaper travel sections, penny-saver circulars, travel catalogues, AAA and Michelin travel guides, travel brochures, travel magazines.

Write the following questions on the chalkboard: "If cigarettes cost $3.00 a pack, and someone smokes one pack a day for a year, how much will smoking cost that person over the course of a year?"

• **INTRODUCE/MODEL** Distribute Reproducible 42 to each student. Read the question written on the chalkboard while the students read along on their papers.

Ask what the question means. Break the question into its three dependent clauses. Have early- and intermediate-production students pantomime each clause, then act out the full question. Brainstorm how they might solve the problem.

Have a volunteer write down the possible solutions. Help the students develop a formula for their problem. Then, solve the problem together.

• **TEACH/PRACTICE** Distribute various travel realia. Make sure students understand the directions

for Part 2 of Reproducible 42. Challenge the group to plan an exotic vacation with the amount of money saved by not smoking, using the travel information. Encourage them to stay within their budget. Remind them to allow for travel costs, food, incidentals, housing, souvenirs, and perhaps suntan lotion.

Have early-production students cut pictures from brochures and glue or tape them to poster board to illustrate their plans. Instruct them to label each item and cost. Check for understanding.

• **CONCLUDE/ASSESS** Have each group share their vacation plans and poster with the class.

Invite the class to calculate how much they could save by not smoking over the course of a year, five years, ten years. Have students brainstorm items that they might purchase with their savings.

Write the items on chart paper to become part of your word bank. Invite early- and intermediate-production students to use the words in simple sentences to tell about what they might do with the money they saved.

Group Names _____

Date _____

The Cost of Addiction

✎ **Part 1.** Work as a class.

If cigarettes cost $3.00 a pack, and someone smokes one pack a day for a year, how much will smoking cost that person over the course of a year?

Describe how you would solve the problem: _____

_____

_____

Write a formula to solve the problem: _____

_____

What's your answer?_____

_____

_____

✎ **Part 2.** Work as a group.

If cigarettes cost $3.00 per pack, and a person quit smoking for two years, how much money would that person save? _____

If you used all the money the person in Part 2 saved by not smoking, what kind of trip could you take? Make your plans here: _____

_____

_____

_____

_____

_____

_____

_____

_____

_____

43. Using Math— Save It or Spend It

Acquiring Language Through . . . : Using manipulatives and discussion.

Objectives: To identify and count U.S. currency; to learn and practice the terms *dollar, save, spend,* and *rules.*

Time Required: One class period to organize, then ongoing.

Group Size: Four to six students.

Materials Needed: Reproducible 43 (one per group); play money, representing U.S. currency; a variety of items students would buy for themselves (items from discount stores or your own trash and treasures); adhesive labels for price tags; poster board.

Teaching Process

• **PREPARE** Create a classroom store by displaying items that students will be motivated to buy (sports equipment, school supplies, free time, special outings). Use adhesive labels or colored dots for price tags. Advertise the bigger prizes on poster board.

Purchase play money or make your own. You might cut out a small picture of your face, fix it to real money, and then reproduce it. Copy enough so each student has a stack of bills.

• **INTRODUCE/MODEL** At the beginning of class, hand out a stack of bills to each student. Explain that this is their weekly salary. Immediately have each student write his or her name on the bills. Facilitate a discussion of the U.S. system of work. Brainstorm such words as *salary, paycheck, payroll, bonus,* and *production.* Conclude the discussion by telling students that the items on display are for sale. To purchase them, students must earn money by following the classroom rules. Help students understand that they can also lose money if they break a rule and that they'll receive a bonus if they exceed the standard. Review the classroom rules you've established. Post these on chart paper. Brainstorm other standards and practices you and the students think can make for a better classroom experience. Discuss ways students can go beyond

what you've established (helping a friend with homework, picking up litter).

• **TEACH/PRACTICE** Distribute Reproducible 43. Make sure students understand directions. You might have pre- or early-production students draw a picture to match each way they might exceed the standard and have the more fluent students write the rules, consequences, and rewards.

• **CONCLUDE/ASSESS** Collect and consolidate the lists. Select a mixed ability group of volunteers to pick out the ten most often mentioned rules and the ways to exceed them. (Make sure *you* can live with the rules.) Then have the students average the cost for breaking each rule and the bonus for exceeding the letter of the law, based on the prices listed on the worksheets.

Pick a certain day of the week. (Fridays are always good for this activity.) On the specified day, give each group time to take an inventory of how they succeeded or failed. Have them pay any fines group members owe. Then have them either go shopping with money they've earned or decide as a group to save their money for another week when they have more money to buy more expensive items.

92

Save It or Spend It

✎ List the top five rules you'd like to see followed in the classroom. How much should it cost, in dollars, if you break the rule? Write that in the space provided.

Rule	**Cost for Breaking Rule**
1. _____	_____
2. _____	_____
3. _____	_____
4. _____	_____
5. _____	_____

✎ List the top five ways you can exceed your own standards. How much do you think each is worth as a bonus? Write that in the space provided.

How to Do More	**Bonus Amount**
1. _____	_____
2. _____	_____
3. _____	_____
4. _____	_____
5. _____	_____

44. Communicating with Math— Before, After, and Between

Acquiring Language Through . . . : Using manipulatives, math games, sequencing numbers, and storytelling.

Objective: To understand the words or the relationships *before, between,* and *after*

Time Required: One class period.

Group Size: Five equal groups of students.

Materials Needed: Reproducible 44 (one per group); 3" x 5" index cards; number line.

Teacher-to-Teacher: This activity is recommended for basic language acquisition. If you use heterogeneous groupings, challenge the fluent students by having them act as facilitators. Motivate them by challenging them to bring a good sense of humor and ingenious storytelling to their group work.

Teaching Process

• **PREPARE** Provide a number line, available at teacher supply stores, or make one on a roll of blank cash register tape.

Write the numbers 1 to 100 on index cards. Stack them in order in a deck.

• **INTRODUCE/MODEL** Write the numbers 1 to 10 on the chalkboard. Show students that by adding a zero to each number, they can skip count to 1,000 by tens (1 becomes 10; 2 becomes 20). Then, say the number and have volunteers repeat the name of the number. When you get to 100, add another zero to 10 to make 100. Continue up to 1,000.

Tell students that numbers fall *between*, *before*, and *after* other numbers. Give examples of numbers that occur in relationship by referring to what you've written on the board and asking students to supply numbers that fall either *between*, *before*, or *after* that particular number. Develop a pattern presentation using the number line to practice similar numbers expressed in relationship. Have pre- and early-production students point to and name the numbers. Build sentences using the

numbers and relationship words in sentences. "_____ comes before _____." "_____ comes after _____ but before _____." Ask individual questions, such as: "What is your number between?" "Is the number before _____?" "Is it after _____?"

• **TEACH/PRACTICE** After introducing the lesson, you may wish to use this as a point of entry to generate vocabulary. Have students substitute nouns after the numbers and make sentences: "The 1,000 clowns came before the 30 students."

Distribute Reproducible 44. Make sure students understand the game. Shuffle the deck of number cards. Deal the deck of numbers randomly to each group.

• **CONCLUDE/ASSESS** Invite a member of each group to share their story through storytelling and actions. Assess limited-English students on how well they express numbers in relationships both mathematically and in full sentences. Assess fluent students on how well they work together by adding ingenuity to this activity.

Before, After, and Between

✎ Place the first card number-side up under BETWEEN. Read each number on the rest of the cards. Place each card under the correct word. Does the number come *before* the first number you put down? Does it come *after*?

BEFORE   **BETWEEN**   **AFTER**

✎ Use the numbers in each stack to make up sentences using the number and the words *before*, *between*, *after*. Write or tell a group story using the sentences you made up as guidelines.

45. Communicating with Math— Picture This

Acquiring Language Through . . . : Using manipulatives, game playing, and generating math terms.

Objective: To use pictorial methods to communicate mathematical ideas.

Time Required: One class period.

Group Size: Partners or small group.

Materials Needed: Reproducible 45 (one per group); drawing paper (eight sheets per group); colored markers; prizes for the class—from school supplies to free time.

Teacher-to-Teacher: This activity works well across the curriculum. Use it either to introduce vocabulary or to assess concepts students have learned. When you need to provide context clues for the words, revisit the relevant activities in this book as well as in the students' own texts.

Teaching Process

• **PREPARE** Make one copy of the reproducible for each group. Cut up the words into cards to make a deck of word cards for each group. Arrange each deck in the same order.

• **INTRODUCE/MODEL** Introduce students to this game by telling them you are going to draw a picture to represent what is written on a word card. Choose one of the easier word cards from the stack. Do not let students see what's written on it. Model the activity using stick figures and simple artwork. Draw the word on chart paper. Have students try to guess what you draw. Once the students figure out what your picture symbolizes, verify their responses by showing them the correct word card. Help them talk about how they arrived at the responses. You might show them how words and pictures go together using a page from a simple picture book. Cover the picture. Read the words. Have students describe the meaning of the words. Then show the picture. Make the point that we need pictures to symbolize words. With early-production students, you may wish to review the words before they play.

• **TEACH/PRACTICE** Explain to the class that they will play a game to help reinforce math terms, based on the game Pictionary™. You might show a

dictionary so that students understand the wordplay of "pictionary" and "dictionary." Review the process for playing the game as follows.

1. Each group is a team. Each member of the team takes a turn as illustrator.

2. Give each team a deck of cards with the words face down, sheets of drawing paper, and markers.

3. Have the first illustrator in each group pick the same card from the top of the deck.

4. Have each team work together as quickly as possible to guess what word the illustrator is trying to draw.

5. The first team to shout out the correct word wins applause from the other groups.

6. Groups play the game until all word cards have been drawn from the deck and illustrated.

• **CONCLUDE/ASSESS** Assessment is built into the game itself. While students are drawing or guessing words, assess their facility at interpreting the word-symbol relationships. Make a big deal about rewarding prizes. Use the opportunity to generate vocabulary by naming items you reward.

Picture This

✎ **Teacher directions:** Reproduce this page and cut terms into cards. Add other math terms you want to review.

order	before	after
between	negative number	timetable
number line	positive number	

IV. Thinking and Communicating in Science and Technology

46. General Science—
Safety First

Acquiring Language Through . . . :   Discussion, drawing, and generating science vocabulary.

Objective: To establish safety rules.

Time Required: One class period followed by periodic review of safety procedures.

Group Size: Four to six students.

Materials Needed: Reproducible 46 (one per group); safety goggles; lab apron.

Teaching Process

• **PREPARE**   Prepare a facsimile of Reproducible 46 on an overhead transparency or large chart.

• **INTRODUCE/MODEL**   Put on a pair of safety goggles and a lab apron to create a sense of intrigue! On the board, write *dangerous* and *safe* in large letters as two column headings. Have your pre- and early-production learners go around the room and point to lab equipment or act out situations that are 1) dangerous and 2) safe when studying science and/or conducting scientific experiments. Chart the vocabulary words in the appropriate column under *dangerous* or *safe*. Add any new words to create a classroom word bank.

Review the rules listed on Reproducible 46 and model for the students how to illustrate one of the lab safety rules.

• **TEACH/PRACTICE**   Have students use Reproducible 46 in small groups to draw pictures illustrating each of the rules listed. They should also try to think of one or two new rules that are not on the list that they think are important.

• **CONCLUDE/ASSESS**   Ask each group to report their new safety rules to the class. You may use the pictures to assess how well second-language learners understand the lab safety rules. Have pre- and early-production learners type in all the safety rules on the computer and compile a class safety book.

Have those students who are bilingual type up the rules in a language other than English so non-English speakers know the rules as well.

Group Names _____

Date _____

Safety First

✏️ Read each safety rule and draw a picture of yourself and/or your classmates following the rule. Add other rules to the list that you think are important

Use tongs or test-tube holders to handle hot test tubes.

Always point test tubes away from you and your classmates when you are heating them.

Do not hurt live animals. Be gentle, please!

If chemicals get in your eyes, use the Emergency Eyewash System and flush them out completely.

Always wear your lab apron.

Wear long hair pulled back when doing experiments involving flames.

Wear safety goggles to protect your eyes.

Never mix or taste chemicals.

Always report accidents or emergencies to your teacher right away.

61 Cooperative Learning Activities in ESL

47. Life Science— Plants and Animals

Acquiring Language Through . . . : Using pictures and total physical response.

Objective: To name plants and animals.

Time Required: One class period. (This activity can be ongoing throughout the school year.)

Group Size: Four or five students.

Materials Needed: Reproducible 47 (as many as necessary); magazine picture(s) depicting plants and animals.

Teaching Process

• **PREPARE** Gather pictures that include both plants and animals from magazines, newspapers or your own photo collection. (Recruit other teachers to help by posting a note and collection box outside the classroom.) Choose two similar pictures for modeling.

• **INTRODUCE/MODEL** Write *Plants* and *Animals* on the chalkboard.

Examine a picture with the class. Identify which living things are plants and which living things are animals. Write the names on the chalkboard in the appropriate column. Then display a second picture. Point to a plant or animal in the picture. Ask, "Is this a _____?" If students agree, have them put their thumbs up. If not, have them put their thumbs down. Continue until they recognize the plants and animals.

• **TEACH/PRACTICE** Hand out as many copies as necessary of Reproducible 47 and several pictures of plants/animals to each group. Make sure students understand the directions. Go from group to group to make sure the names and spellings are correct.

This activity works well for a homogeneous ESL group. If you work with language-proficient students, invite them to take the role of group leader and have them ask questions in the way you have modeled.

• **CONCLUDE/ASSESS** Have each group send an expert from their group to another group to use their flash cards and pictures to teach the other group. Post the picture(s) on a bulletin board. Use the flash cards as labels as well as a teaching tool to work with individuals who need further practice.

Plants and Animals

Categorize each picture your teacher has given your group as either a plant or an animal.

Use the boxes on these pages to make a flash card for each plant or animal in your group's pictures. Draw a picture of each plant and animal inside the box and write its name on the reverse side.

ANIMALS   ## PLANTS

48. Life Science—Eat Them Up!

Acquiring Language Through . . . : Drawing, labeling, and generating vocabulary.

Objective: To recognize, draw, and label commonly eaten fruits and vegetables.

Time Required: One class period.

Group Size: Four to six students.

Materials Needed: Reproducible 48 (one copy for each group); a variety of fruits and vegetables (see classifications on Reproducible 48); salad bowl; paring knife, vegetable peeler, cutting board; salad dressing; paper bowls; plastic forks; napkins.

Teaching Process

• **PREPARE** Purchase or collect fruits and vegetables from the school food service that represent each category on Reproducible 48.

Wash and display them. Make a flash card or sentence strip for each item.

• **INTRODUCE/MODEL** Point to each fruit and vegetable. Name each and show its flash card or sentence strip. Have students repeat the names.

Explain that today's activity involves grouping each fruit or vegetable into the four categories on the reproducible. Display Reproducible 48 and go through it point by point. Check for understanding by repeating the ideas or concepts frequently.

As you go through and explain each category, point to and name examples of each category among the fruits, and vegetables you have on display.

For example:
leafy vegetables: lettuce
root vegetables: carrots
stems: celery
fruits: tomatoes

• **TEACH/PRACTICE** Have students work in groups to classify the rest of the fruits and vegetables on display using Reproducible 48. Encourage them to match characteristics using the written information provided as well as by seeing and handling the items. If possible, repeat use of the reproducible at a grocery store or farmers' market. Have students fill out one reproducible while they shop.

• **CONCLUDE/ASSESS** Ask each group to share their findings with the whole class.

Cut up the fruits and vegetables and make and toss a salad. Give everyone their own sample and compare and contrast the different tastes and textures.

Eat Them Up!

✎ List and draw in the boxes the fruits and vegetables that match each category.

Leafy vegetables: have green leaves. Produce food by photosynthesis.

_____

_____

_____

LEAFY VEGETABLES

Root vegetables: round or narrow, with some root hairs left on them. Usually hard. Some require cooking before eating. Absorb nutrients and water from the soil.

_____

_____

_____

ROOT VEGETABLES

Stems: usually slender stalks above-ground. Carry water and nutrients to the leaves, which are usually green. Produce food by photosynthesis.

_____

_____

_____

STEMS

Fruits: part of the plant's reproductive system. Usually contain seeds or beans in order to grow more plants. Promote the scattering and germination of seeds.

_____

_____

_____

FRUITS

49. Life Science—Make a Face

Acquiring Language Through . . . : Labeling, total physical response, and generating vocabulary.

Objective: To recognize parts of the face.

Time Required: One class period.

Group Size: Partners.

Materials Needed: Reproducible 49 (one for each student); colored marking pens; hand mirrors.

Teaching Process

• **PREPARE** Prepare an overhead of Reproducible 49.

• **INTRODUCE/MODEL** Surprise the class by making a crazy face. Ask them to describe what you did. For example, stick out your *tongue*, raise your *eyebrows*, or wiggle your *ears*.

Explain that everyone will draw the face that you just made. Model this drawing process on the overhead of Reproducible 49. As you draw each part of the face, ask each student to touch that part of his or her face. After students complete their faces, review the vocabulary by pointing to the facial features and naming them again. Use more difficult anatomical labels such as *jaw, cheeks, forehead,* and *brow* to continue the activity.

• **TEACH/PRACTICE** Give a copy of Reproducible 49 to each student. Pass out the hand mirrors. Have students work with a partner to draw their own faces on the reproducible and label the parts based on the new anatomical vocabulary they've learned or reviewed. Partners should assist each other with vocabulary and facial details.

• **CONCLUDE/ASSESS** Collect the drawings and shuffle them. Pass out the portraits and have students guess whose face they are holding. Assess second-language learners' language acquisition. As students show their drawing, ask them to point to or name the different facial features.

This activity must be approached with sensitivity. If you have special-needs students with facial malformations, you may need to adapt this activity.

Reproducible 49

Make a Face

 Draw a face here as your teacher gives you directions, and label the parts.

 Now, use a mirror to draw your own face here, and label the parts. Let your partner help you.

50. Physical Science—
People in Science

Acquiring Language Through . . . : Cloze activities, role-playing, discussion, and generating science vocabulary.

Objective: To learn about famous scientists through reading from context.

Time Required: One class period.

Group Size: Two to three students.

Materials Needed: Reproducible 50 (one per group); classroom word bank or dictionaries (one for each group).

Teaching Process

• **PREPARE** Simply make copies of Reproducible 50 and proceed.

• **INTRODUCE/MODEL** To model a cloze exercise, where students use meaningful context to complete or fill in the word that is missing from a text, write the following sentence on the board:

"Learning new vocabulary helps us grasp new ideas. Successful _____ need to understand new _____ or scientific terms."

Also write a list of possible vocabulary words that students might use to fill in the blanks. Substitute *students* or *scientists* for the first blank and *words* or *vocabulary* for the second blank. Read the sentence aloud and pause when you come to the missing word. Tell the students that any of these words or phrases would make the sentence correct and that sometimes we need to substitute our own words for a word we do not know.

• **TEACH/PRACTICE** Give each group a copy of Reproducible 50. Brainstorm a classroom word bank or use a dictionary. Have groups complete the cloze exercises. Ask fluent English speakers to read the sentences, pausing when they come to a missing word/phrase, so that other students can call out words from context and the recorder can write them down.

• **CONCLUDE/ASSESS** Once students have completed the cloze exercises, have each group brainstorm things each of the famous scientists might say. For example, Madame Curie might say, "I have discovered radium!" or "At last, a woman is recognized as a famous scientist."

Encourage early-production students to act out the part.

People in Science

✎ Complete the following sentences in your own words. There is no right or wrong answer as long as the entire paragraph makes sense.

1. Marie Curie was born in 1867 and died in 1934. She was a French _____ best known for her discovery of radium. Together with her husband, Pierre, she _____ the 1903 Nobel Prize for physics, and she _____ the Nobel Prize for chemistry in 1911.

2. George Washington Carver was a black American _____ who helped the poor people in the southern United States. He was born a slave on a Missouri farm. He _____ scientific experiments and found that peanuts and sweet potatoes both improved the soil and grew well in the South. His fame as a _____ grew throughout the world, and when he died on June 5, 1943, he was one of America's most _____ scientists.

3. The German-American _____ Albert Einstein was the scientist who most shaped the twentieth-century vision of physical reality. After World War I, Einstein's _____ —especially his theory of relativity—received more public attention than any other scientific idea. Early in his life, he failed an important exam, and no one thought he would become the _____ man he is known as today.

✎ Write things that each of these scientists might say.

Marie Curie might say:

_____

_____

George Washington Carver might say:

_____

_____

Albert Einstein might say:

_____

_____

Acquiring Language Through . . . : Total physical response, use of manipulatives, lab experimentation, and generating science vocabulary.

Objective: To understand the molecular movement of temperature.

Time Required: One class period.

Group Size: Four to six students.

Materials Needed: Reproducible 51 (one for each group); various thermometers—e.g., basal (oral, rectal, and/or under-the-arm), ear, outdoor; two clear plastic cups or bowls for each group; food coloring for each group; hot and cold water; poster board.

Teaching Process

• **PREPARE** Gather the materials necessary for this activity and display the different types of thermometers. Heat a large pan of water. Have on hand a cold pan of water.

• **INTRODUCE/MODEL** Show an outdoor thermometer and a basal thermometer you might use at home. Brainstorm with students and list everything they associate with the word *temperature*. Map all the adjectives on a word web, making sure to include *hot*, *cold*, *warm*, *lukewarm*, *chilly*, *sizzling*, and *freezing*. Create a word bank from this session.

Have language-proficient students explain *temperature*. If necessary, tell students it is a measure of hot or cold. Explain that heating something makes the temperature rise. As something cools off, its temperature falls. This is accomplished by the movement of tiny molecules, minuscule particles that everything is made of. Show this by placing a thermometer in hot water.

• **TEACH/PRACTICE** Have students use Reproducible 51 in groups to record their findings as they conduct an experiment to see what happens to the molecules of water when the water is hot. For each group, fill one cup or bowl with hot water and the other cup or bowl with cold water. Remind students about the safety precautions for handling hot water.

Ask that a student carefully pour a drop of food coloring into the middle of each cup or bowl. Have the groups observe and discuss how the molecules move the food coloring around the cup or bowl.

• **CONCLUDE/ASSESS** Invite groups to report their findings to the rest of the class. Discuss their responses to the questions on the reproducible.

Chart their findings on a large sheet of paper. Do a group edit as you check for accuracy and evaluate the scientific findings. This class dictation can be illustrated by pre- and early-production learners and made into an observation poster. Use this poster and the word bank to generate and practice vocabulary.

Turn Up the Heat

EXPERIMENT:

> Fill one container with hot water. Fill the other with cold water.
> Carefully pour a drop of food coloring into each container.

✎ What do you see?

• Write about it.

_____

_____

_____

• Draw it.

• Think about it.

✎ Why does the food coloring disperse more rapidly in hot water and more slowly in cold water?

_____

_____

✎ If you heat the water, what happens to the temperature? Why do you think this happens?

_____

_____

✎ What might cause the rapid movement in the hot water?

_____

_____

52. Earth Science— Biome Sweet Biome

Acquiring Language Through . . . : Research, drawing, and discussion.

Objectives: To label illustrations; to provide and practice oral and written descriptions.

Time Required: Three to five periods.

Group Size: Five groups of students.

Materials Needed: Reproducible 52 (one per group); construction paper; scissors; magazines about nature and animal life; masking tape; thumbtacks; stapler; colored marking pens; natural artifacts such as sand, water, dirt, and grass.

Teaching Process

• **PREPARE** Prepare an overhead transparency of Reproducible 52. Collect various magazines with vivid drawings and photographs of terrestrial biomes, including forests, grasslands, and deserts.

Gather art supplies to help students design a classroom terrestrial biome exhibit.

Select materials and organize a classroom research and reading area to include science text-books, science books, encyclopedias, and Internet documents about terrestrial biomes.

• **INTRODUCE/MODEL** Explain that the students' job will be to design an exhibit of a terres-trial biome, including:

• Tundra (arctic and alpine)

• Coniferous Forest (U.S. Northwest)

• Temperate Deciduous Forest (foothills and lower slopes of eastern North America and Europe)

• Tropical Rain Forest (Amazon basin of South America; Congo basin of Africa, Southeast Asia)

• Grasslands (Great Plains of North America, Argentine pampas, the Serengeti in Africa, the steppes of Asia, grasslands of Australia)

• Desert (U.S. Southwest, northern and southern Africa, Australia, the Middle East, South Amer-ica's Atacama, China's Gobi)

Point out an example of each biome on the classroom map. Acknowledge any newcomers who may be from or near that geographic area.

Select one biome to model for the class. Go step by step through the overhead. Build a word bank. Use pictures from your classroom research. First, identify and illustrate all the words that students know. Then write down any new words that they don't know. Make word cards for these. Ask intermediate-production students to guess the words from context. Have students look up their meaning. Post the word bank to remind all students and validate what the second-language learners already know.

Have volunteers cut out pictures from maga-zines and draw pictures of the biome you have selected to model and arrange this as the first display.

As a group, write at least three sentences describing the biome. Ask *who*, *what*, and *where* questions about the following.

• Description: **What** it is? **Where** it is located?

• Habitation: **What** people, plants, or animals live there?

• Climate: **What** are the ranges of rainfall and temperature?

52. Earth Science—
Biome Sweet Biome

• **TEACH/PRACTICE** Assign one biome to each group. Encourage students whose native countries are part of a particular biome to work in that group. Distribute Reproducible 52 and all necessary supplies. Make sure that students understand the directions. Use at least one class period for research. Work with pre- and early-production learners who may need to draw and label parts of their biome in order to acquire language. Use at least another period to create the biome.

• **CONCLUDE/ASSESS** Conduct a classroom tour so each group can experience all the terrestrial biomes. You may wish to ask each group to describe or act out a scene depicting their terrestrial biome.

Reproducible 52

Biome Sweet Biome

Our biome: _____

✎ Build a word bank that helps describe your biome: First, write down the words you know. Then, write down the new words.

Word Bank

Words We Know	New Words

✎ Now, get to know your biome by answering the following questions.

_____

_____

Description: What is it? _____

_____

_____

Where is it located? _____

_____

Habitation: What people, plants, or animals live there? _____

_____

_____

Climate: What are the ranges of rainfall and temperature? _____

_____

_____

Use your art supplies to create a classroom exhibit of your biome. Show the features you've identified above.

53. Earth Science—
Pollution Solutions

Acquiring Language Through . . . : Noting and recalling details and solving problems.

Objective: To understand and describe the need to recycle and how it's done.

Time Required: One class period to introduce the activity and one week to complete disposal tracking.

Group Size: Partners.

Materials Needed: Reproducible 53 (one per partner group).

Teaching Process

• **PREPARE** Simply make copies of the reproducible and proceed.

• **INTRODUCE/MODEL** Share the following facts with the students:

Every person in the United States throws away one to three pounds of garbage every day, on the average. Explain to the class that three pounds of meat can feed a family of six to eight people. If possible, display three pounds of meat to give them an idea of how much this is. Americans throw away enough trash in one day to fill 63,000 garbage trucks. Placed end to end these would reach from Philadelphia to Pittsburgh, Pennsylvania.

Pull down your classroom map and show the students how far that really is. Point to your city or town and show the distance to another city or town that is about 350 miles away from you.

Tell the class that some materials can be reused for their original purpose. Brainstorm some ideas for how you might recycle things around your classroom instead of throwing them away. For

example, you might decide to recycle paper by using the other side as scratch paper or to save and recycle the aluminum foil the school lunches are delivered in.

The most obvious example is the beverage container. Used only once and discarded, a can or bottle adds to the solid waste flow; replacing it is costly and increases the pollution caused by manufacturing. A returnable beverage bottle, on the other hand, can average 15 to 20 fillings before breaking.

• **TEACH/PRACTICE** Pass out Reproducible 53 and have students work in pairs to keep track of their disposal methods for a week. This chart should be completed by the pairs as they think of new ways the item can be reused or recycled.

• **CONCLUDE/ASSESS** Have partners compare their disposal charts with others in the class. As a whole class, look for similarities and differences. You may wish to make a comparison chart such as a Venn diagram. Add any new vocabulary words to the word bank.

Partners' Names _____

Date _____

53. Pollution Solutions

✎ Keep track of the trash you throw away for a week. Write the kinds of trash you get rid of in Column 1. Write how it could be reused if you recycled it in Column 2.

1. TRASH	2. HOW IT COULD BE REUSED

54. Technology— Our Technological World

Acquiring Language Through . . . : Cloze activities, role-playing, and generating technological vocabulary through discussion.

Objectives: To learn about the history and application of technological advances; to learn to read from context.

Time Required: One class period.

Group Size: Partners.

Materials Needed: Reproducible 54 (one per partner group).

Teaching Process

• **PREPARE** Simply make copies of the reproducible and proceed with the activity.

• **INTRODUCE/MODEL** First, write the following words on the board and ask students to share what they already know about each one: ***computer, television (TV), electronic mail (e-mail).*** Chart their responses and make a word bank. Let the class know that you will be sharing some more facts about each of these technological advances with them in the next activity.

To model a cloze exercise, where students use meaningful context to complete or fill in the word that is missing from a text, write the following sentence on the board: "Communication is very important. We use technology in order to _____ with each other and improve our _____ in school, at work, and at home." Also write a list of possible vocabulary words that might fill in the blanks. For example, *talk* or *communicate* could fill in the first blank and *work* or *communication* could fill in the second blank. Read the sentence aloud and pause when you come to the missing word. Tell the students that any of the suggested words would make the sentence correct and that sometimes we need to substitute our own words for a word we do not know.

• **TEACH/PRACTICE** Ask students to use Reproducible 54 as they work together in pairs to complete the cloze exercises. They can use the classroom word bank or dictionary to complete the sentences about technological advances. It works well to pair more proficient English speakers with pre- or early-production learners. Ask the fluent English speaker to read the sentences, pausing when she/he comes to a missing word/phrase, so that the other student can call out words from context. Have the student who reads the sentences also chart the words that will complete the cloze activity.

• **CONCLUDE/ASSESS** When all pairs have finished the cloze exercises, ask each pair to brainstorm things each of the technological advances might do to help make our lives easier. For example, a computer in school might enable a student to type reports and fix mistakes easily.

Next, invite each pair to say or act out one thing that one of the technological advances might do to help them in their daily lives. Encourage students to use the brainstorm list or to think of a new idea that has not been mentioned. Gather around by moving chairs into a circle or sitting on the floor so pairs of students can share their technological advances with the rest of the class.

Our Technological World

Complete the following sentences in your own words. There is no right or wrong answer as long as the entire paragraph makes sense. You may use the classroom word bank or dictionary if you wish.

1. A computer is a _____ built to help us think quickly and easily and solve _____ . By the 1990's, many people were using computers in their homes to do many things, such as _____ .

2. The development of modern color television took place in the United States during the late 1940's. The groundwork began in 1930, when an American, Frank Gray, _____ a way to use color channels. In 1938, the Frenchman Georges Valensi developed the idea of a color system that would work with black-and-white technology. Most _____ in America did not have color televisions until after 1964.

3. Electronic mail, or e-mail, refers to messages that are _____ from computer to computer over ordinary telephone lines. A user of electronic mail needs a _____ to send messages to another person.

55. Technology—What's My On-Line?

Acquiring Language Through . . . : Collecting artifacts and the media.

Objective: To understand different jobs that require computer use.

Time Required: One to two class periods. Allow one week to collect artifacts as a follow-up activity.

Group Size: Groups of four to six students.

Materials Needed: Reproducible 55 (one per group); job listings from classified sections of the newspaper; various computer-related artifacts or realia related to a teacher's job; a tote bag, briefcase or something similar in which a teacher might carry his or her job-related necessities.

Teaching Process

• **PREPARE** Select various objects that suggest how computers help you do your job as a teacher (e.g., computer disk, lesson plan computer print-out). Place these in your choice of carrying case.

• **INTRODUCE/MODEL** Share the computer artifacts you brought in that relate to your job as a teacher. Take them out of your briefcase or bag one by one. Have students name them. You might have pre- and early production students act out what you do with them. Label each item.

• **TEACH/PRACTICE** Pass out Reproducible 55. Assign each group one of the jobs listed on the reproducible. Have them research the job. They should use the classified section of the local news-

papers, research books, periodicals, encyclopedias in the library, and job listings from the Internet or from local employment offices.

It is now the students' job to come up with computer-related artifacts and to design or find an appropriate carrying case that a person would use on that particular job. For example, a secretary might carry a tote bag filled with computer disks, a computer printout such as a weekly calendar, and an e-mail communication.

• **CONCLUDE/ASSESS** Host a "What's My On-Line?" artifact exhibit for other classrooms. Give a guided tour of the realia students bring in, along with an explanation based on the research.

What's My On-Line?

✎ Research the job that your teacher assigns to your group. Then, come up with computer-related items or artifacts that a person doing the job might use. Design a carrying case that fits the person doing the job.

✎ Collect your artifacts, fill your carrying case, and share it at your "What's My On-Line?" artifact exhibit.

JOB DESCRIPTION #1:

Secretary FT, admin. and computer skills, good typing. Fax résumé.

JOB DESCRIPTION #2:

Writer with computer experience, must have excellent communication skills and a "team" attitude. Call 555-1000.

JOB DESCRIPTION #3:

Bank teller PT, basic loan knowledge required, fluency in spoken and written English and Chinese, word processing and spreadsheet necessary. Send résumé.

V. Health, Wellness, and Safety and Prevention

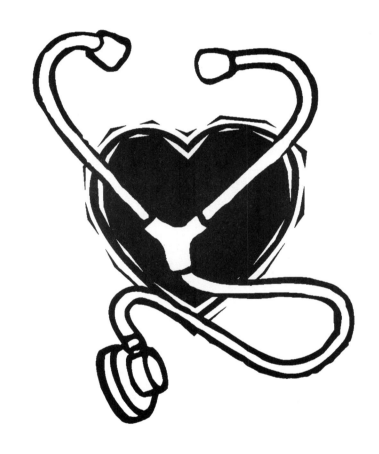

56. Health—Food for Thought

Acquiring Language Through . . . : Using the media and total physical response.

Objectives: To recognize the names of common foods; to evaluate grocery shopping in terms of the common food groupings.

Time Required: One to two class periods.

Group Size: Five or six students.

Materials Needed: Reproducible 56 (one per group); packages and samples of real food; pictures and ads from food magazines, newspaper food supplements, and grocery store flyers; a copy of the food pyramid, including explanations of exactly what constitutes a serving of each food group.

Teaching Process

• **PREPARE** Bring samples of a variety of food containers, boxes, and wrappers to class. Check with the school cafeteria, grocery store, and other teachers to help gather a large supply.

Display pictures and ads from food magazines, newspaper food supplements, and grocery store flyers.

Find the food pyramid in health books or on packages of food such as grocery bags, milk cartons, and bread wrappers. Enlarge any of these and make it into an overhead.

• **INTRODUCE/MODEL** After telling students that they will explore how to recognize, choose, and buy foods that fulfill their nutrition requirements, divide the class into groups of five or six. Assign each group a sequence of letters from the alphabet (*A–F, J–M,* etc.). Provide pictures and food ads from newspapers and magazines. Direct each group to cut out pictures of food and advertisements beginning with their letters of the alphabet. Likewise tell them to select packaged goods beginning with the same letters.

Distribute Reproducible 56. Introduce or review the food pyramid as shown in your classroom display. Refer to the reproducible to check students' understanding of food groups and servings. Work together to fill in the first column, "What Food to Eat?" For each recommended food-group serving in the "Food Groups" column, write a specific food in the "What Food to Eat?" column. For example, breakfast calls for one serving of fruit, so in Column 1, you could write "1 banana" or "glass of orange juice." Have second-language learners make flash cards for those items they don't know.

• **TEACH/PRACTICE** Have the students work in groups to fill in Columns 2 and 3. Students should be as specific as possible in Column 2—for example, "Oakhurst orange juice, 1 quart." Tell students to look at the print material (ads, fliers) in order to compare the price listings in Column 3. Work with individuals learning English to practice using the names of foods as you ask them questions: "What cereal would you buy?" "How much does spaghetti cost?"

• **CONCLUDE/ASSESS** Compare what each group purchased. You might categorize and assess the work by looking at the foods by cost, by most enjoyable menus, by healthy choices, by money best spent. Whenever possible, draw from your experience as a consumer to help the students.

Group Names _____

Date _____

Food for Thought

✎ How would you feed your family?

✎ Look at the food groups listed. Use each serving to plan a menu in Column 1. Look at Column 1 to plan what food you must buy in Column 2. Check the newspaper and supermarket ads to find out how much the food would cost, and write the price in Column 3.

Food Groups	1 What Food to Eat?	2 What Food to Buy?	3 How Much Does the Food Cost?
BREAKFAST milk, yogurt, or cheese (1 serving) fruit (1 serving) bread, cereal, rice, or pasta (3 servings)			
LUNCH milk, yogurt, or cheese (1 serving) fruit (1 serving) bread, cereal, rice, or pasta (3 servings) meat, poultry, fish, dried beans, eggs, or nuts (1 serving) vegetables (2 servings)			
DINNER milk, yogurt, or cheese (1 serving) fruit (1 serving) bread, cereal, rice, or pasta (3 servings) meat, poultry, fish, dried beans, eggs, or nuts (1 serving) vegetables (2 servings)			

57. Health— Read the Label

Acquiring Language Through . . . : Semantic mapping, discussion, and reading food labels.

Objectives: To use adjectives to describe how foods look and taste; to express preferences.

Time Required: One class period.

Group Size: Partners or four students.

Materials Needed: Reproducible 57 (one per group); pickle slice or another food of your choice (one per student); several packaged foods with "Nutrition Facts" on the labels; wax paper; napkins or paper towels.

Teacher-to-Teacher: This activity can lead nicely into any nutrition unit. You may use it to analyze the food pyramid or talk about sodium and cholesterol content in terms of students' diet or what foods are provided in the school lunch program. Or you may compare student preference for one food or another. Show these comparisons on a Venn diagram and plot them on a bar graph.

Teaching Process

• **PREPARE** Provide several packaged foods, one to two per group. Choose foods with distinctive tastes and textures (sweet, sour, salty, crunchy, soft, liquid).Organize work spaces to assure sanitary conditions, including setting up napkins and wax paper for each group.

Prepare an overhead of any "Nutrition Facts," which appear on all food labels. Provide visuals for items included in the "Nutrition Facts," "such as *serving size*, *servings per container*, and *percentages*. Prepare an overhead of Reproducible 57 or write a facsimile of it on the chalkboard.

• **INTRODUCE/MODEL** Point to each food you've displayed. Identify and name the food aloud. Write it on chart paper and retain this as a word bank. For background, you may need to explain: "In a normal 2,000-calorie diet, a person should not consume more than 65 grams of fat, 2,400 mg of sodium, and 300 mg of cholesterol in a day." Refer to the overhead of "Nutrition Facts." Have volunteers help define the terms in the "Facts." Use visuals to shelter the teaching. Give examples or display things that represent terms such as *serving size*, *servings per container*, and *percentages*.

Now give each student a pickle slice or food of choice. Display the overhead of Reproducible 57

or refer to the copy of it on the chalkboard. Model, then have volunteers provide adjectives to describe the pickle slice. You might fill in sample sentences using the adjectives, such as:

"This tastes (spicy, hot, sour)."

"This looks (rough, bumpy, small)."

• **TEACH/PRACTICE** Hand out copies of Reproducible 57. Make sure students understand the directions. Distribute sample foods to each group. Have them look at, taste, and describe the foods, then fill out the reproducible.

Ask students to point out what is included in the "Nutrition Facts" and the listed ingredients for their food. Help students match the descriptions they've written on the reproducible to appropriate items in their food's "Nutrition Facts" or ingredient list. For example, if a student says the food is sweet, he or she should look for sugar, honey, or Nutrasweet™ in the "Nutrition Facts" or the ingredients list.

• **CONCLUDE/ASSESS** Compare each group's findings. Evaluate how the second-language learners can identify foods—first naming them, then describing them.

Read the Label

Name your food: _____

 Describe how it looks and tastes.

Our food looks like:

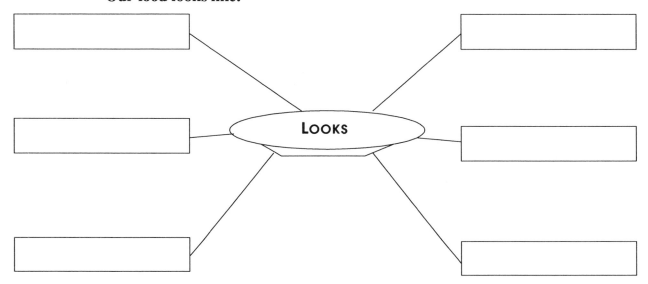

LOOKS

Our food tastes like:

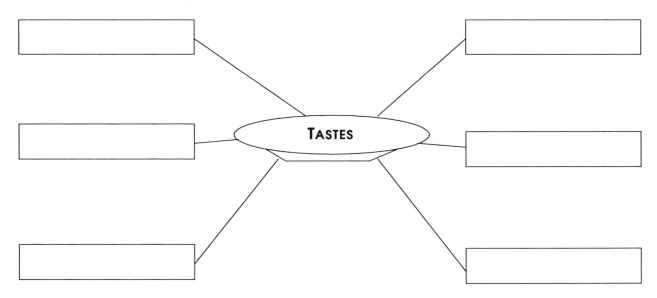

TASTES

58. Wellness—Sick and Tired

Acquiring Language Through . . . : Total physical response, drawing, and conversation.

Objective: To describe ailments and accidents.

Time Required: Two class periods.

Group Size: Partners.

Materials Needed: Reproducible 58 (one per person); an anatomy chart or large picture of a person; clear overhead transparencies.

Teaching Process

• **PREPARE** Display an anatomy chart or a large picture of a person.

• **INTRODUCE/MODEL** For a warm-up, quickly go through a review of parts of the body. Make a game of pointing to parts of the body on the visuals you've displayed and on yourself, and then have the students point to parts of their own bodies.

Model for them a sample speech about an accident or illness relating to a body part: "I was not in school this week. I [point to arm] broke my (arm)."

Continue, but change past tense to present tense and interchange subjects. (Refer to Reproducible 58 for more examples.) As you fill in the sentences, write any new words on an overhead.

Then invite volunteers to act out being sick, each time modeling a sample speech and listing all new words.

• **TEACH/PRACTICE** Use another transparency. Draw a simple picture of yourself when you've been sick or had an accident. Have students guess what is wrong with you, using simple sentences.

Direct partners to Reproducible 58. Make sure they understand the directions.

• **CONCLUDE/ASSESS** Have students cut out their pictures from the reproducible. (Be sure they put their names on the back of each.) Shuffle these and distribute the pictures to the class. Have volunteers guess the illness or accident. Assess how well students discuss ailments, accidents, and physical feelings.

Sick and Tired

✎ Work in partners to complete this activity.

Underline at least three statements below that tell how you felt when you had an illness or an accident.

Talk to your partner about how you felt.

I have a fever.	I have an earache.	I am sick and tired.
She has a toothache.	He broke his foot.	You have a cut on your face.
You broke your arm.	His throat is sore.	She sprained her wrist.
Her eyes were red.		

✎ Draw two pictures of yourself described in any of the statements on this page. Then draw one picture of another illness or accident.

✎ Write three or four simple sentences below to describe one of these times when you were sick or injured.

_____

_____

_____

_____

_____

59. Wellness—A Hop, a Skip, and a Jump

Acquiring Language Through . . . : Total physical response, games, and generating vocabulary.

Objective: To understand warm-up or aerobic exercise for physical education in terms of direction, time, and effort.

Time Required: One class period.

Group Size: Two to three students for practice, small groups to conclude.

Materials Needed: Reproducible 59 (one per group); clear overhead or butcher paper; rhythm music (optional).

Teacher-to-Teacher: It may be necessary to modify the movement activities in order to include physically challenged students.

Teaching Process

• **PREPARE** Prepare a word bank on an overhead or on butcher paper of the following words used in warm-ups and aerobic exercise (include others you may be familiar with): **stretch, bend, touch, twist, sway, lift, march, reach, step.**

• **INTRODUCE/MODEL** Invite students to participate in a warm-up or aerobic exercise activity, asking one of the more rhythmic students to provide a drumbeat or another student to be a DJ and play a cassette tape or rhythm track. Have the students follow along as you show how the exercises are executed. Point out each word on the word bank before you demonstrate it. Use those words in combination with direction words: "Stretch right," "Bend left," "Lift up." Have students repeat the

words and actions with you. Make it like a gym routine or aerobics class.

• **TEACH/PRACTICE** Divide the class into groups. Distribute Reproducible 59. Make sure students understand the directions.

Direct each group to develop their own exercise routine, using the reproducible as a guide.

• **CONCLUDE/ASSESS** Have the students perform their exercise routine. If you are not the physical education instructor, invite that person or a coach to evaluate the routine and point out proper technique.

A Hop, a Skip, and a Jump

WRITE A LIST OF WORDS THAT TELL DIRECTION.

_____   _____

_____   _____

_____   _____

DRAW A SIX-STEP EXERCISE ROUTINE. (USE STICK FIGURES.)

1.	2.	3.

4.	5.	6.

WRITE SHORT INSTRUCTIONS FOR YOUR EXERCISE ROUTINE.

1. _____   4. _____

2. _____   5. _____

3. _____   6. _____

60. Safety and Prevention—
The Sports Page

Acquiring Language Through . . . : Total physical response, word games, and using the media.

Objectives: To acquire language in order to foster participation in physical activities, sports, and play; to evaluate safety rules and precautions for physical activities.

Time Required: Two class periods.

Group Size: Three to five students.

Materials Needed: Reproducible 60 (one per group); physical fitness, health and sports magazines; sports equipment, particularly safety gear; sentence strips or index cards for flash cards; writing paper; construction paper.

Teaching Process

• **PREPARE** Set up a learning center with physical fitness, sports, and health magazines. Display sports equipment. Make flash cards to label the equipment as necessary.

• **INTRODUCE/MODEL** Write the words *sports* and *play* on the chalkboard. Have students brainstorm all the sports, games, and other physical activities they like to play or attend.

Write and maintain the words on the chalkboard or chart paper to use as a word bank. Invite pre- and early-production students to act out responses.

• **TEACH/PRACTICE** Divide students into small groups. Give a copy of Reproducible 60 to each group. Have students find each activity in the word search puzzle and circle it. Make sure students understand how to find words across and down. Regroup and add any new words to those you've brainstormed.

Review the word bank list of activities. Have students discuss the kinds of things and equipment they need to participate safely in each activity. Help

the discussion by selecting recreational and sports activities from the word bank that require special safety precautions (in-line skating, bicycling, swimming, baseball). Refer to the materials in the learning center for additional prompts.

Divide the class into small groups again. Assign a different sport to each group. Have them write safety rules and precautions for their assigned sport.

• **CONCLUDE/ASSESS** Supply each group with writing paper. Have them write up or use a computer to publish their safety rules and precautions.

Encourage second-language learners to select pictures from the classroom display of magazines or to illustrate their writing. Bind these rules together into a book.

Have each group use the displayed safety equipment and the book to prepare a sports safety exhibit. Evaluate all students on group effort and on individual use of English for second-language learners.

Group Names _____

Date _____

Reproducible 60

The Sports Page

Find the sports activities listed below in the word search grid. Circle each one. Words may go across or down.

1. hiking	6. tennis	11. surfing	16. football
2. aerobics	7. basketball	12. jogging	17. bicycling
3. fishing	8. hockey	13. track	18. dancing
4. walking	9. soccer	14. swimming	19. golf
5. baseball	10. skating	15. volleyball	20. bowling

b	o	w	l	i	n	g	a	v	k	x	c
d	a	n	c	i	n	g	h	o	w	r	t
v	b	a	s	e	b	a	l	l	a	j	m
b	a	s	k	e	t	b	a	l	l	u	c
t	e	n	n	i	s	l	d	e	k	f	q
r	n	g	h	o	c	k	e	y	i	i	s
a	s	o	c	c	e	r	z	b	n	s	o
c	u	l	j	d	x	l	f	a	g	h	j
k	r	f	o	o	t	b	a	l	l	i	o
p	f	t	b	i	c	y	c	l	i	n	g
b	i	d	s	w	i	m	m	i	n	g	g
g	n	s	k	a	t	i	n	g	y	r	i
f	g	a	e	r	o	b	i	c	s	m	n
a	e	i	o	u	y	h	i	k	i	n	g

61 Cooperative Learning Activities in ESL

61. Safety and Prevention—
The House That Love Built

Acquiring Language Through . . . :   Poetry and total physical response.

Objectives: To identify parts of speech; to analyze the causes and effects of illegal drugs within a community; to evaluate pro-social behavior.

Time Required: One to two class periods.

Group Size: Three to four students grouped by mixed ability.

Materials Needed: Reproducible 61 (one per group); art supplies; large paper for making big books.

From the Bookshelf: *The House That Crack Built*, by Clark Taylor, illustrated by Jan Thomas Dicks. Chronicle Books, 1992.

Teacher-to-Teacher: You may adapt this activity by substituting "The House That Jack Built" in Activity 15. Insert the word *Love* for the name *Jack* in the title and break up the poem by verses. However, by using the suggested reading, you have many points of entry that are powerfully relevant.

By using current newspaper articles about drug busts or gang-related activity, you can make parallels with the book. Ask students to identify people and places in the news article that could be either the cause or effect of what the reading describes.

Teaching Process

• **PREPARE**   For classroom use only, reproduce the pages in *The House That Crack Built* that are assigned for each group on Reproducible 61. You may either photocopy the illustrated pages or take apart the book and laminate the illustrations.

• **INTRODUCE/MODEL**   Revisit or introduce the poem "The House That Jack Built," Reproducible 15. After reading *The House That Crack Built*, post an enlarged version of Reproducible 61. Write the word **house** on the chalkboard. Ask students to describe their lives if they lived in the house that crack built. Encourage pre- and early-production students to act out different scenarios. Chart the responses by clustering them around the word *House*.

• **TEACH/PRACTICE**   Distribute the page of *The House That Crack Built* indicated on the reproducible to each group. Have the students brainstorm the words circled on their page in the story-poem and then brainstorm what it would be like if the drug

problem did not exist. They must substitute the indicated word with an alternative word(s), as if they were retelling their page from the point of view of living in a place where houses are built with love.

Work independently with limited-English students, going word by word. Replace such words in the title as *The* with other pronouns; *House* with names of other things; *Crack* with healthy food or activities. Have students act out, read, chant, or rap each time you put a new word in place.

• **CONCLUDE/ASSESS**   Have the students share their responses. As a class, do a group edit of the poem, substituting new words and situations for those circled. Challenge them to depict a community at peace, one that supports alternatives to drugs. Entitle this "The House That Love Built." Invite students to illustrate each page of their poem. They may also create a rap with choreography and present this along with the book to other classes.

Group Names _____

Date _____

The House That Love Built

✎ Look at your assigned page. Use the circled words as a starting point. Brainstorm all the words that you might think or feel if you were a kid who lived in that place pictured. Write those words in the lines below.

What if everything changed and this was a place where love ruled? Brainstorm what it would be like in that world without drugs. Rewrite your page, substituting words to make the sentence positive and healthy.

Group 1

This is the man who lives in the house that crack built.

_____

Group 2

This is the drug known as cocaine.

_____

Group 3

This is the boy feeling the heat.

_____

Group 4

This is the girl killing her brain.

_____

Group 5

And these are the tears we cry.

_____